AT THE
Headwaters

The 1993 Flood in Southwestern Minnesota

40 Photos and

40 Essays

Joseph Amato and
Janet Timmerman
EDITORS

1995

MCC

South
west
State
University
Marshall, Minnesota 56258

Distributed in the United States of America by the Society for the Study of Local and Regional History,
Box 291, Marshall, MN 56258-0291

Cover photograph by Jerry Sowden; back cover photograph by Lois Winter

This material is based upon work supported by the Corporation for National and Community Service under
Grant No. 94spfmm006 awarded to the Minnesota Conservation Corps for Special Programs for Flood Relief.

This publication was made possible in part with funding from the Minnesota Humanities Commission in cooperation
with the National Endowment for the Humanities and the Minnesota State Legislature.

ISBN 0-9614119-9-6
Printed and bound in the United States of America

Dedication

This book is dedicated to Thaddeus Radzilowski
who understands what a university
should mean to the people it serves,
and to the people of this region whose fate
is not to be separated from its waters.

"The flood of 1993 was the result of an unwitting alignment between the forces of nature and the civil works of humans."

–Richard E. Sparks

Table of Contents

Acknowledgements _____

This is a book of many authors and many sources. Thus, considerable gratitude is owed. Thanks first go to the five student flood historians, each of whom wrote on a different subject. Toni Beebout-Bladholm, who gathered the photographs for this book, examined the floods in light of people's personal experiences. Jennifer Mathiason looked at the way the floods revealed class differentiation in the city of Marshall. Stacy Monge studied the divergent points of view and interests of agencies that regulate water and administer flood relief. Julie Porter studied the causes and effects of the flood on Pipestone, a city on the west side of the Coteau des Prairies. Rebecca Schlorf dedicated her attention to the effects of the floods on agriculture and wildlife, and produced the bibliographic essay in this book. Janet Timmerman, an AmeriCorps/VISTA volunteer and former Southwest State University history student, served as the group's supervisor. She knitted the students into the community, while helping edit and design the book. At the same time, she dedicated herself to describing the region's hydrology and drainage.

Regional writer, Howard Mohr; Southwest State University writers and professors, Bill Holm and David Pichaske; and Mankato State University historian, Charles Piehl, contributed essays to this book, as did former Southwest State history student, Janet Liebl. *Marshall Independent* reporter Jim Muchlinski not only contributed essays but his time as well, to help the students in their research efforts.

David Monge did a yeoman's job of copy-editing the book in its most primitive form. John Radzilowski did the final copy-editing of the book and offered valuable contributions to its design. Kathy Wenzel of Livewire Printing turned our wishes into a book design and saw the book through its final publication.

Our gratitude is considerable to all those who offered valuable technical advice and information. This includes Dallas Lindgren and Jon Walstrom from the Minnesota Historical Society; John Afinson, Terry Engel, Ken Gardner, Wayne Knotts, Dave Loss, Dave Raasch, Kent Spading, Ferris Chamberlain, and Ben Wopat from the Army Corps of Engineers, St. Paul District; Rose Anderson and Merle Behrens from the Lyon Soil and Water Conservation District; Jeanine Antony, Jeff Buessing, and Loretta Penske from Western Community Action; Mike Appel and Mike Monsey from the Soil Conservation Service; Tom Behm from the Minnesota Department of Transportation; Stephanie Bethke from Southwest Veterinary Services; Bret Anderson, Pat Baskfield, Kerri Christoffer, Tom Hovey, Larry Kramka, and Ogbazghi Sium from the Department of Natural Resources; Ellayne Conyers from the Lyon County Historical Society; Charlie Cook and Maria Gomez from the Minnesota Department of Human Services; Bob Finley from the Redwood-Cottonwood Rivers Control Area; David Frey and Bob VanMoer from the Marshall Wastewater Treatment Plant; Rick Goodemann from the Southwest Minnesota Housing Partnership; Todd Hammer and Dave Robley from the Lyon County Highway Department; Harvest States Cooperatives; Jeff Holcomb from the Agricultural Stabilization and Conservation Service; Linda Julien from the Red Cross; Leo Langer, Cottonwood Agricultural Consultant; Betty McSwain from the Pipestone National Monument; Harlen Nepp, Pipestone County Emergency Management Coordinator; Susan Ude from the Minnesota Housing Finance Agency; Kerry Netzke from Area II Minnesota River Basin Projects; Ann Peterson from the Southwest Regional Development Commission; Paul Otto from Camden State Park and Rick White from Split Rock Creek State Park; Greg Payne and Lee Trotta from the United States Geological Survey; Shirley Peotter from the Western Human Development Center; Tony Straussar from the Southwest Minnesota Experiment Station; attorney Kevin Stroup from Clarkfield; Bill Swope, Eastside and Westside Elementary School principal; Charlie Trautwein from Earth Resource Observation Systems; Tammy VanOverbeke, Lyon County Civil Defense Director; and Richard Victor, Marshall City Engineer. Special thanks are extended to Marshall Mayor Robert Byrnes, who was most generous in satisfying our many requests which included tours of the affected area and critical appraisal of parts of this work in its early stages.

Others who generously offered personal information about their experiences with the floods include: Jeanne Blomme, Mrs. Alex Burczek, Joe Buysse, Richard and Diane Cady, Helena Carlson, Florence Dacey, Chuck Derby, Bev Haynes, Monte Kiple, Jan Kraft, Gail Peavey, Tom Pofliet, Shirleen Schwab, Mary Swander, Richard VanderZiel, James and Marianne Zarzana, David and Pat Zwach, and regional farmer Loren Piehl, who was the first to contact us and guide us through the uplands.

We also extend our gratitude to the following individuals, organizations, and newspapers who furnished us with information and photographs for this book: Chad Been, Minnesota Department of Natural Resources, Dorothy Gransey, *Jackson County Pilot,* Dale Kreft, Lyon County Engineers Office, Lyon County Historical Society, Minnesota Historical Society, Arloene Olson, Charles Piehl, *Pipestone County Star, Redwood Gazette,* Julie Porter, Schwan's Sales Enterprise Inc., Jerry Sowden, Jean Stockwell of the *Marshall Independent, Tracy Headlight Herald,* and independent photographer Lois Winter.

Of course, our gratitude would be incomplete without giving thanks to those from Southwest State University whose support and encouragement was consistent and generous. First and foremost, our thanks go to former Associate Vice President for Academic Affairs, Thaddeus Radzilowski, and former Southwest State University President, Oliver Ford, both of whom conceived and wrote the original grant. Vice President of Academic Affairs, Randy Abbot, assisted and enthusiastically encouraged us in many ways. Also, thanks to Charles Myrbach of Institutional Grants and Research, who ably helped us initiate and administer the Flood Project; and Interim-President Douglas Sweetland was encouraging. Others gratefully to be remembered at the university are Rural Studies Coordinator, Donata DeBruyckere; Director of University Relations, Bill Turgeon; Director of the Southwest Regional History Center, Janice Louwagie; Jeff Kuiper, Mary Mortland, Deb Kerkaert, and Jan Van Moorlehem from the University Business Office; Gwen Beebout, History Department secretary; Dorothy Frisvold, Social Sciences secretary; Shawn Hedman, Academic Computer Coordinator; Brian Schmiesing, Professor of Agribusiness Management; Elizabeth Desy, Associate Professor of Biology; John Bowden, Library Director; and Dicksy Howe, Librarian.

Finally, special gratitude is owed to members of the Minnesota Conservation Corps, who supported this book in many important ways. Director of the Minnesota Conservation Corps, Larry Fonnest, administered the grant in a positive spirit, and in the same spirit, Flood Recovery Coordinators, Mark Robbins and Jesse Roberts, helped us implement the grant.

–Joseph Amato
April 20, 1995

Preface

Joseph Amato

In the Bible it rained forty days and forty nights. With forty essays and photos, *At the Headwaters* evokes the memory of the 1993 flood in southwestern Minnesota. It will not be easy to forget the 1993 flood, especially for those who lost land and crops and those who were driven out of their homes.

As with all events, the majority of people will reduce the flood to a few simple memories. Some have already transformed the 1993 flood (which in southwestern Minnesota was three different floods) into a few memorable incidents and stories.

Even during the flooding, few grasped the multiplicity of the flood's forms and effects. Some floods are local, some regional, and some national. Some come from heavy rains in a single place, others flow from saturated or frozen ground that holds no water, and others from broken dams.

As difficult as it is to grasp the diverse origins of floods, it is even more complex to determine with any accuracy the degree to which floods are creations of nature and creations of man. Yet, the historians of the Flood Project had to do this when they reconstructed the floods of 1993.

Composed of one history teacher, one VISTA worker (who had studied history), and five students (only one of whom had studied history), the Flood Project historians have been intent on preserving and enlarging our memory of the 1993 flood in southwestern Minnesota. Housed at Southwest State University and working under a federal flood grant to the Minnesota Conservation Corps of the Minnesota Department of Natural Resources, they have focused on the origins and effects of the 1993 flood, especially in and around the regional lead city of Marshall.

To preserve the history of the 1993 flood, the flood historians have collected photographs and documents, and interviewed select individuals and representatives of agencies concerned with the flood. These materials will be stored as part of a permanent collection at Southwest State University's History Center, which is a branch of the Minnesota Historical Society. Additionally, with the support of the Minnesota Humanities Commission, they planned a two-day conference on the 1993 flood. And they wrote this account of the 1993 flood.

In writing this book they recognized that, along with shared memories, there is a community of interest in flooding among the people of southwestern Minnesota. Settled on and at the base of the Coteau des Prairies, the glacial moraine of southeastern South Dakota and southwestern Minnesota, flooding has been a recorded problem since agricultural settlement a century ago. Forming a vast, high, and natural collecting unit (once pocketed with sloughs, bogs, lakes, and wetlands), the Coteau des Prairies formed a unique watershed disbursing waters to the Minnesota, Missouri, and Red Rivers. Standing some 600 feet above the prairie, the Coteau des Prairies' escarpments—ever more drained and tiled—disburse its waters more directly and rapidly to the floodplains below. Its waters flow in all directions: to the east its rivers flow to the Minnesota River; to the south to the Des Moines River, then across Iowa, to the Mississippi; to the south and west to the Rock River that flows to the Big Sioux, then on to the Missouri, which joins the Mississippi at St. Louis; and to the north to the Bois des Sioux River, which joins the Red River of the North and ultimately flows into Hudson Bay.

That the Coteau is the source of so many rivers accounts for the title of this book, *At the Headwaters,* and was the source of the assumption that southwestern Minnesota serves as a regional microcosm of the 1993 national flood, the greatest flood of the upper Mississippi River valley in this century. In studying the floods of southwestern Minnesota, the flood historians believed they would understand much about flooding in the other headwaters that made this great flood. They looked for a part of the explanation that made the 1993 flood in conjunction of a great meteorological event and a century of channeling, drainage, and tiling in the Mississippi's upland. They discovered that the 1993 flood revealed much about twentieth-century national efforts at water control, something that every agricultural and industrial society carries out.

"I do not know much about gods; but I think that the river is a strong brown god."
—T. S. Eliot

However, these interests did not make *At the Headwaters* an academic book. It does not have a thesis or make a single argument. Its intention was as much to evoke the flood as to analyze and explain it. The impressionistic and popular character of the book is testified to by the heterogeneous nature of its forty essays, as well as the order of the essays themselves. We begin the book with a general characterization of the flood of 1993, contrasting it with preceding floods. Before commenting on the effects of the flood in the region and the city of Marshall, we characterize the land and waters of southwestern Minnesota. The book concludes more philosophically, reflecting on what the 1993 flood taught us about our control of water at home and in the nation. At every point, we hope *At the Headwaters* is an invitation for the reader to remember and think about the 1993 flood.

The Great Flood of 1993

Joseph Amato

The Flood of 1993 was without precedent. In terms of precipitation, record river levels, area of flooding, and economic losses, it surpassed, according to a government report, all previous floods in the United States.

The Flood of 1993 was not one flood but many floods. The floods occurred at many places throughout the upper Midwest during the late spring and summer of 1993. Places flooded once were often flooded again, and then again.

Although most floods are the product of a single storm or spring snow melt and runoff, the 1993 flood resulted from numerous intense thunderstorms for the most sustained period in history throughout the whole upper Mississippi.

In Iowa (at the heart of the storms), from January to September, 54 inches of rain fell. The rain made for the wettest period in 121 years of national weather record keeping. The rain fell at a time of heavily saturated soils, and of the greatest cloud cover and the lowest evaporation rate in national history.

Throughout the summer the whole nation watched weather satellites relay photographs of a jet stream stalled over the upper Midwest like, in the words of *Iowa's Lost Summer*, "a lid on a mason jar." The high pressure system over the eastern part of the country pumped moisture-laden air from the Gulf of Mexico north. That air bumped into the jet stream and down came the rains, torrential rains of 5, 9, and even 15 inches at a time. Across the Midwest swollen streams fed swollen creeks that fed swollen rivers which converged to make the century's greatest flood of the upper Mississippi valley.

The 1927 flood, the century's greatest flood of the lower Mississippi, broke levees, destroyed cities, and wiped farms and homes off the floodplain. It killed as many as a thousand people and left approximately a million and a half homeless. The 1993 flood killed only 47 people and left 74,000 homeless. Nevertheless, from an economic point of view, the U.S. Army Corps of Engineers judged it to be "the most devastating flood in the history of the United States."

It caused $15 to $20 billion in damage. Approximately 70,000 private homes were washed away or severely damaged, while between 35,000 and 45,000 commercial structures were damaged. Farmland and crop losses were counted in millions of acres. (It affected almost seven million acres of farmland in Minnesota alone.) Cities were overrun, highways and shipping lanes closed, levees destroyed, and river banks and channels severely eroded.

In nine Midwestern states—Iowa, Missouri, North Dakota, Wisconsin, Minnesota, South Dakota, Nebraska, Kansas, and Illinois—505 counties were declared eligible for

| **Federal Disaster Area Counties by State** | | |
State	# of Eligible Counties	% of State's Counties
Iowa	99	100
Missouri	85	75
North Dakota	39	74
Wisconsin	48	67
Minnesota	53	61
South Dakota	39	59
Nebraska	52	56
Kansas	51	49
Illinois	39	38
Total	**505**	

–U.S. Army Corps of Engineers, *The Great Flood of 1993 Post-Flood Report: Upper Mississippi River Basin,* September 1994

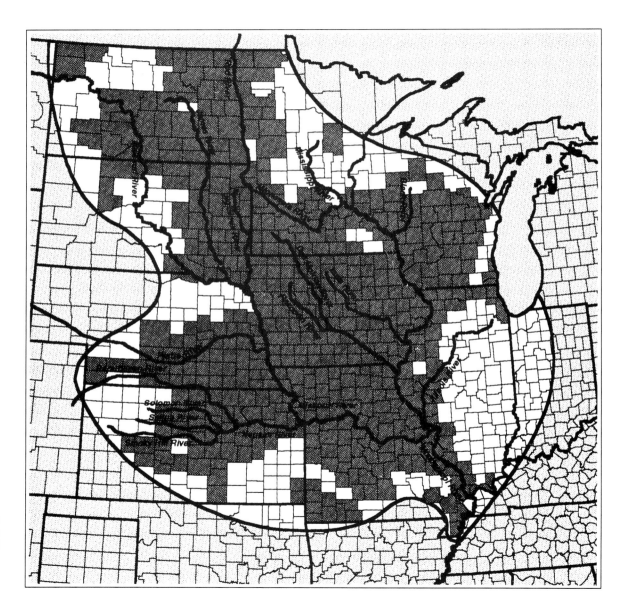

Flood-affected counties which received Federal disaster assistance

–*The Great Flood of 1993:*
The Minnesota Experience. St. Paul:
Minnesota Department of Public Safety, 1994

federal assistance. At the top of the list was Iowa; all 99 of its counties were eligible.

The flood taught the American people many things. It taught about natural powers. It also highlighted the nation's great resources to predict, cover, and cope with floods. From satellites to helicopters, from civil defense to government agencies to insurance, the nation—which had done a lot to help cause the flood—also went a long way toward mitigating and civilizing the flood.

As if tailoring some of its lessons for ecologists and naturalists, who were no longer forced to sit at the back of the national classroom, the flood showed that floodplains are meant for flooding and flooding is required for the renewal of plants, birds, and fish.

The flood also renewed what was known as "the great river debate." The scale and damage of the flood, naturalists contended, was the result of a mania of draining, channeling, and levee building that had ruled the development of the entire upper Mississippi basin for the last hundred

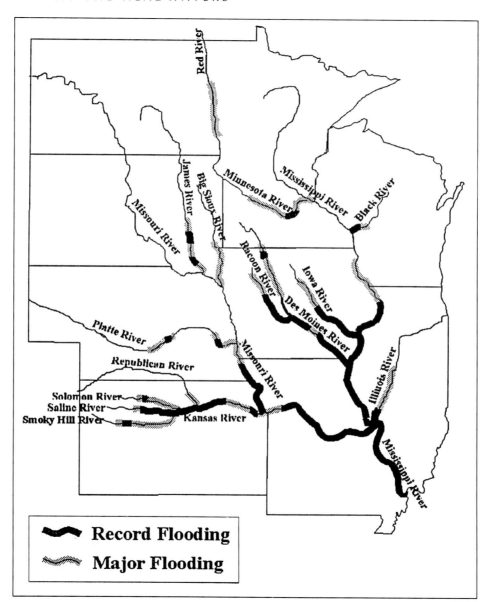

Major rivers flooded in 1993

–U.S. Department of Commerce, NOAA, National Weather Service

5

years. With every agricultural and urban area intent on getting rid of its own excess waters, while protecting itself against its neighbors' descending waters, channels were dug ever deeper and straighter, and levees raised higher. The rivers of the basin, like the Mississippi they feed, became artificial troughs carrying more and more water. The valley's uplands composed of vast wetlands, chutes, backwaters, and side channels that once absorbed water and the floodplains that once expanded to hold excess runoffs have been eliminated. Consequently, waters quickly gather from headlands and uplands to form great floods.

> *"Nothing under heaven is softer and more yielding than water, but when it attacks things hard and resistant there is not one of them that can prevail."*
>
> −Laozi

The point of the naturalists' argument, like the conclusion to all serious contemporary arguments, was political: Congress must protect wetlands, reform flood insurance to discourage floodplain development, and promote water and soil conservation on farms. Appearing to have the force of the century's largest flood on its side, the argument could not simply be put aside. The flood had exposed the price of floodplain development. Furthermore, taxpayers were sick of paying for floodplain and farm bail out. Even the major federal report, *Sharing the Challenge: Floodplain Management into the 21st Century* (The Galloway Report) registered the need for rethinking on the part of the government and the Army Corps of Engineers.

There is, however, no clear sign yet that a new order of thinking will amount to a new order of acting. There is much to keep the old way intact. It is present, not future, political constituents who need and insist on immediate help. It is old levees that needed to be rebuilt and raised and new levees and channels that promise relief from future floods. Even more compelling in maintaining the old way is the simple fact the nation has fed itself and grown strong by the control of its waters. It is hard to believe that one flood, however great, could dissuade the Midwest—the heartland and feedbag of the nation—from its hitherto immensely successful policy of drain and channel.

Nevertheless, if awareness is the goal of the good teacher, the flood of 1993 was a great teacher of the nation. It taught on great scale that the motives and interests that divide citizen from citizen and nation and nature are as deep and long as the rivers they share.

Summary of Events

Stacy Monge

March–April	Spring flooding begins. Rapidly melting snow and heavy spring rains saturate the ground.
April 17	Residents of Grafton, Illinois, are forced from their homes by the rising Mississippi.
April 22	Illinois Governor Jim Edgar declares Grafton a disaster area.
April 28	Missouri Governor Mel Carnahan declares a state of emergency in St. Charles County.
May 6–19	The "Mother's Day" flood hits southwestern Minnesota, wiping out farmers' first planted crops of the season.
May 6	High winds, tornados, and severe rainstorms cause extensive damage near Balaton, Florence, and Marshall, Minnesota.
May 7	The Split Rock Creek earthen spillway collapses, severely flooding Split Rock Creek State Park near Jasper, Minnesota.
May 8	The American Red Cross opens an emergency shelter at East Side Elementary School in Marshall.
May 13–14	Minnesota Lieutenant Governor Joanell Dyrstad surveys the damage in Marshall and Federal Emergency Management Agency officials tour the area to assess the regional damage.
May 15	Final planting date for small grains.
June 5	Ending date for planting corn.
June 7	Lyon, Murray, Pipestone, and Rock counties in Minnesota are included in a tornado watch. Tornado-like winds hit the area and cause extensive damage in Tracy, forcing 89 residents to flee the Frog Alley mobile home park and seek shelter at the Tracy National Guard Armory.
June 10	Deadline for planting soybeans.

June 11	President Bill Clinton approves assistance for Brown, Cottonwood, Lincoln, Lyon, Murray, Nobles, Redwood, Rock, and Pipestone counties.
June 14	The disaster field office opens in Marshall.
June 15–23	The "Father's Day" flood hits southwestern Minnesota. Farmers again lose crops as a result of flooding in combination with accompanying cool weather.
June 17	Federal and state agencies conduct an organizational meeting to coordinate relief efforts.
June 18	Minnesota Governor Arne Carlson and agriculture officials tour Minnesota. The Redwood River peaks at 15.73 feet near Redwood Falls, Minnesota.
June 19	The Cottonwood River peaks at 18.87 feet near New Ulm, Minnesota.
June 21	The Yellow Medicine River peaks at 10.84 feet near Granite Falls, Minnesota.
June 20–26	Governor Carlson decrees 28 Minnesota counties to be in a state of emergency.
June 25	Coast Guard officials close a 215-mile stretch of the Mississippi River from Bellevue, Iowa, to Canton, Missouri. A four-year-old boy drowns after falling into the swollen Redwood River near Lynd, Minnesota.
June 25–28	Area farmers turn to aerial planting of soybeans as a last ditch effort to get a crop in the ground.
June 29	The United States Department of Agriculture approves emergency haying and grazing.
June 29–30	The Interagency Hazard Mitigation Team tours Minnesota.
June 30	U.S. Secretary of Agriculture, Mike Espy, tours the area.

July 1–4	The "Independence Day" flood hits southwestern Minnesota.
July 2	The Federal Emergency Management Agency declares Yellow Medicine and five other counties eligible for assistance.
July 6	United States agricultural policies are extended or adjusted to meet the needs of hard-hit farmers.
July 9	Seven more Minnesota counties are added to the list of those eligible for assistance.
July 10	About 600 people are evacuated from the small town of Adrian, Minnesota, as floodwaters overtake their homes. The Mississippi River peaks at 27.15 feet in Keokuk, Iowa.
July 12	Senator Paul Wellstone and Representative David Minge meet with area farmers at Mike's Cafe in Marshall.
July 14	President Clinton publicly introduces a $2.5 billion aid package to help cover the costs of cleaning up the flood-damaged Midwest.
July 16	The Federal Emergency Management Agency opens a disaster aid center in Marshall.
July 17	President Clinton meets with the governors of Illinois, Iowa, Minnesota, Kansas, Missouri, Nebraska, North Dakota, South Dakota, and Wisconsin to discuss relief efforts.
July 18	The Mississippi River reaches 46.9 feet in St. Louis, Missouri.
July 23	Lac Qui Parle and two more Minnesota counties are declared eligible for assistance.
July 27	The U.S. House of Representatives passes a $3 billion flood-relief package.
July 28	The Southwest Minnesota Private Industry Council announces the availability of funds for emergency employment as part of a $1 million grant to the Minnesota Department of Jobs and Training.
August 1	The Mississippi River peaks at 49.97 feet in St. Louis, Missouri.
August 6	The U.S. House of Representatives passes a $5.7 billion spending bill.
August 8	The Minnesota River crests at 16.46 feet in Montevideo, Minnesota.
August 12	President Clinton signs the $5.7 billion Disaster Supplemental Bill.
August 15	Austin, Minnesota, floods along the Cedar River.
September 15	Last day to designate crops for the 0/92 program.
November 15	Last day to apply for Federal Emergency Management Agency Assistance.

Not One Flood, But Three

Toni Beebout-Bladholm

In the national memory, the flood of 1993 will be transformed into one great hydrological event—perhaps the century's greatest on the upper Mississippi. In the memory of the people of southwestern Minnesota it was three separate floods: the Mother's Day flood, the Father's Day flood, and the Independence Day flood.

The source of the Mother's Day flood was a great meteorological event of winds and waters that reached southwestern Minnesota on May 7, 1993. The storm resulted from an area of low pressure over Colorado, with both warm and cold fronts colliding and stalling over the Midwest. Preceded by winds of tornado velocity, rain saturated the area. The storm itself was the first flood-producing event of the season, setting off many more to come. Its high winds, first felt in Russell, flattened a vacant trailer home, destroyed a double garage, and ripped the roof off a tavern in Florence. Many other buildings in the path of the storm were also destroyed. The following day, May 8, large hail accompanied by heavy rains struck in a band from Tyler to Tracy. A funnel cloud touched down in Balaton, demolishing numerous buildings. Rain continued to pour down on southwestern Minnesota, finally letting up on May 10. On that day the Redwood River was running at 16.5 feet, approximately 2.5 feet above crest level.

The localized nature of this event confined the severe flooding to the upper Redwood River and Cottonwood River basins, distinguishing it from the major Minnesota River flooding that occurred a month later. Heavy rain fell in a period of a few hours. In only six hours, Florence received 5.15 inches of rain. Similar amounts fell in Canby, Montevideo, Jackson, Worthington, Dawson, Marshall, Balaton, Milroy, Redwood Falls, and Tracy. The communi-

Camelot Trailer Park residents evacuating

—Jerry Sowden,
Marshall Independent

ties that suffered most were closest to the Redwood and Cottonwood rivers.

The Father's Day flood of June 15–18 caused further damage. In contrast to the Mother's Day flood, the heaviest rain of the Father's Day flood fell downstream from Marshall. The Mother's Day flood was created in a few hours, while the Father's Day flood was created by several days of rainfall. The rains hit Jackson on June 23, at which point the community had already received 7.32 inches of rain.

The Independence Day flood was the third and last flood of 1993 in southwestern Minnesota. It arose from a strong weather pattern that developed over Nevada and Utah. Like the Mother's Day flood, the Independence Day flood was created by heavy rainfall in a short period of time. For example, Russell received 4.30 inches of rain in a 12-hour interval. Like the Mother's Day flood, the Independence

Day flood had no concentrated area of rainfall; however, it did involve the same band of communities.

"The summer of 1993 produced three of the five greatest recorded flood discharges on the Redwood River at Marshall, Minnesota," said Ferris Chamberlain of the Army Corps of Engineers.

Despite the fact that the three floods all occurred within two months and caused a single period of misery for the people of the region, they were the result of three separate weather events that should not be lumped together.

"As I wipe the moistened glass, I see nothing but water, pattering on the deck from the lowering clouds, dashing against the window, dripping from the willows, hissing by the wheels, everywhere washing, coiling, sapping, hurrying in rapids, or swelling at last into deeper vaster lakes, awful in their suggestive quiet and concealment."
—Bret Harte

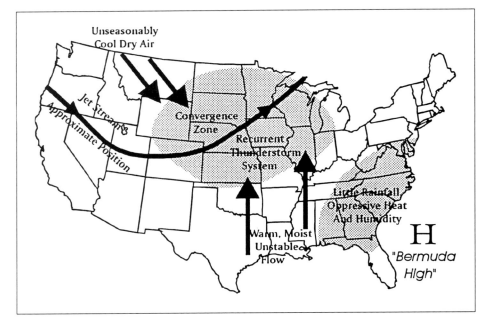

Weather pattern, June–July 1993
—U.S. Department of Commerce, NOAA, National Weather Service

Two Great Floods; Two Different Experiences

C. H. Piehl

The Lower Mississippi River Flood of 1927 and the Upper Midwest Floods of 1993 were both massive disasters affecting countless people and causing loss of life and property over millions of acres of the mid-section of the nation.

Although separated by two generations, these major floods shared many characteristics. They brought major disruption to both rural and metropolitan areas, providing an example of shared experience for people living in very different geographical regions. They inundated floodplains on which towns and farms had been built despite preceding floods.

New developments in transportation and information technology in the years prior to both floods helped spread news of each throughout the nation, stimulating interest in and expressions of relief from people far from the floods. In the case of the 1927 flood, the changes included widespread use of maneuverable seaplanes and motor boats that enabled access to areas isolated by the flood. Small, portable cameras with film had been developed that could capture dramatic views of the effects of the flood from land and air. In the 1993 flood, hundreds of helicopters not only helped in dramatic rescues, but also made it possible for video cameras to send live images to large media networks linked by satellites, which themselves sent photographs of the floods back to earth.

During both 1927 and 1993 citizens and public officials made great efforts to portray the events as a cohesive instead of divisive social experience. At the same time, other citizens expressed the belief that some victims brought their fate upon themselves by ignorant, selfish, or even evil actions that endangered or injured others, including the rescue workers.

1927 Red Cross plea for flood victims
–American Red Cross

Nonetheless, important changes made the 1993 flood a different experience from the 1927 flood. The same technology that enabled rapid spread of news in the 1993 flood brought improvements in weather forecasting and communications, which enabled advanced warnings that doubt-lessly saved lives and property. It also made possible mobilization of resources to assist in evacuation and relief much more rapidly than had been the case in 1927.

CANADA

RICHMOND TIMES. DISPATCH BROOKINS
7/93

UNITED

MISSISSIPPI RIVER

TES

PACIFIC OCEAN

MEXICO

GULF OF MEXICO

ATLANTIC OCEAN

–Reprinted with permission from Gary Brookins

In the course of the 1993 flood, local, state, and especially federal government agencies provided services that significantly affected the lives of virtually everyone in the flooded region. Such services were intended to meet all sorts of individual and group needs, preventing, planning for, and providing assistance after the floods. Despite substantial disdain for large governments, sizeable government bureaucracies were an important and visible part of most people's lives in good and bad times. Unlike 1927, when the secretary of commerce was dispatched by President Calvin Coolidge to mobilize relief efforts following the flood, in 1993 both public and private agencies were in place to act even before disaster struck.

Changes and growth in governmental structure and programs between 1927 and 1993 have created a "revolution of rising expectations." People have come to expect that solutions could be provided to most, if not all, crisis situations. Government agencies were expected to keep floods from occurring, provide assistance, as well as prevent abuse of social programs for flood survivors in the aftermath. Instead of taking active responsibility for relief, top governmental officials—from President Bill Clinton on down to state legislators—showed their concern for the victims of the 1993 flood by making sure that the many levels of bureaucracy below them did their job. How could it be otherwise when big floods are met by big governments?

In the Shadow of the Ridge

Janet Timmerman

Minnesota is defined by water. "Minnesota" means "sky-tinted water." The state's history and development are directly tied to its hydrology. Its first inhabitants, the Native Americans, used the waterways and lakes for transportation and food, as did the first European adventurers and traders. Commerce began along lake and river shores, and agriculture started along the river valleys and out into the prairies. Three-quarters of Minnesota's boundaries are made up of waterways, and the state is home to the headwaters of the nation's mightiest river, the Mississippi.

The southwestern corner of the state is the source of one of the state's most important river systems, the Minnesota. Southwestern Minnesota also straddles the watershed divisions of the Mississippi and Missouri rivers and borders the headwaters of the Red River. At the heart of this area lies the Coteau des Prairies, an ambling ridge six to nine hundred feet higher than the surrounding plains. Named Buffalo Ridge for the great herds that once roamed its slopes, it stretches northwest to southeast across the boot heel of Minnesota. Tens of thousands of years ago glaciers moved down from the north pushing with them massive amounts of rock and debris. As the glaciers melted and receded they left that debris behind, creating a high moraine on top of a deep layer of pre-glacial quartzitic bedrock. The glacial drift covers the bedrock in a layer from 200 to 600 feet thick. Glacial meltwaters carved the ravines and waterways down which streams still flow.

Four of the streams that originate on Buffalo Ridge are important tributaries to the Minnesota River and resemble one another in their hydrology. The Lac Qui Parle, Yellow Medicine, Redwood, and Cottonwood rivers all rise from the uplands of the Coteau, falling quickly from the steep escarpment on the east side of the ridge. All of these rivers drop several hundred feet to the plain below, where the terrain levels out and the streams begin a long, slow fishtail across the prairie before they cascade down into the valley of the Minnesota River. At the base of the ridge, where each stream reaches the prairie floor, it

> *"Knowing rivers, you know the slope and the bias of the earth's body. You know how the land lies."*
>
> –Conrad Hilberry

creates a natural floodplain between the rushing upstream waters and the slower downstream segment. All of the streams have narrow watersheds that run parallel to one another. This creates a unique drainage pattern that favors spillovers from one watershed to another in times of high rainfall. The four streams together drain approximately 3,500 square miles of Minnesota. Add to that the other tributaries that run directly into the Minnesota, and the total area drained amounts to over 4,600 square miles.

The Des Moines River, which has its source at Lake Shetek on the eastern slope of Buffalo Ridge, cuts a slow path southward across the southcentral part of Minnesota and flows dark with the turbid runoff from efficiently-drained agricul-

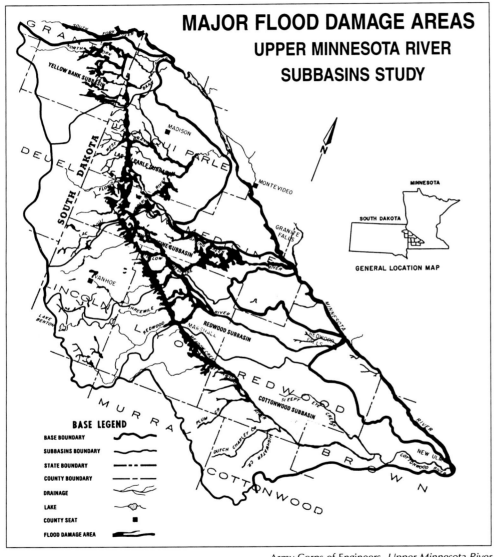

MAJOR FLOOD DAMAGE AREAS
UPPER MINNESOTA RIVER
SUBBASINS STUDY

GENERAL LOCATION MAP

BASE LEGEND

BASE BOUNDARY	
SUBBASINS BOUNDARY	
STATE BOUNDARY	
COUNTY BOUNDARY	
DRAINAGE	
LAKE	
COUNTY SEAT	■
FLOOD DAMAGE AREA	

–Army Corps of Engineers, *Upper Minnesota River Subbasins Study (Public Law 84-639),* 1980

tural land. It drains approximately 1,500 square miles of Minnesota before meandering into Iowa to become one of that state's largest rivers.

Buffalo Ridge divides the Mississippi and Missouri watershed basins. The streams that run from its western and southern exposures have a different hydrology from their northeastern siblings. They lack the extreme initial drop and flow more gently away from their source, due to the absence of steep ravines on the western side. The Rock River is the only main tributary of the Missouri River to flow from Minnesota. Others, such as Pipestone and Split Rock Creeks, flow into South Dakota's Big Sioux River and then on to the Missouri.

The eastern side of the ridge holds many wetlands and poorly-drained areas, whereas the western side, deemed the dry side, has few potholes and even fewer lakes. Although this should create dissimilar patterns of flooding, residents on both sides suffer frequently from too much run-off when the ridge sends down its excess water, like it did during the flooding of 1993.

Fire and Flood: The Pipestone Experience

Julie Porter

At 4:30 P.M. on May 7, 1993—Mother's Day weekend—it began to rain in Pipestone, Minnesota, and did not stop until 1:00 A.M. the following morning. Four inches of rain fell that night. This downpour was preceded by a rainfall of 1.41 inches Thursday night, causing major flood problems in the city of Pipestone. Water gushed overland on a parallel course to the judicial drainage ditch causing the initial flooding along with surface water flowing from within the city. The flood peaked early Saturday morning in northeast Pipestone, with many businesses and homes reporting damage from the flooding. On the afternoon of Saturday, May 8, the city council met in a special session and declared a flood emergency. On May 9, Governor Arne Carlson declared a state of emergency. On May 11 Pipestone County commissioners passed an emergency disaster declaration.

Although no serious injuries or deaths occurred, one couple had a close call. Firefighters rescued Ray and Elaine Jolitz of Pipestone early Saturday morning after their rented home exploded. Fire Chief Marlin Taubert said the explosion was caused by a freezer compressor, which ignited the gasoline that was floating on the floodwater in the garage. This caused a flash fire that destroyed the home completely.

There were reports of sewage backup in parts of northeast Pipestone and other areas of town. The city's sewer system could not handle the additional floodwater. It went from receiving 600,000 gallons of water a day to between 12 and 14 million gallons of water. Much of the excess water that the sewer system received happened within minutes of the heavy downpour.

Helena Carlson, owner of Fort Pipestone, found 18 inches of water in the building. She could not get inside to view the damage until Sunday after the water had receded. By Tuesday, enough water was gone to allow Carlson to begin

Pipestone Creek flooding the Pipestone National Monument
–Pipestone County Star

cleaning up with the help of volunteers. They worked 16 hours a day. Water that had filled the store was black, muddy, and greasy. Scum had coated everything in the store. Straight bleach was poured onto the wooden floors to cut through the scum, and the bleach had to be scrubbed into the wood several times.

Pipestone had another scare on Monday, June 7. Sirens sounded, though an ominous-looking storm had passed and the sun was shining. Nonetheless, the storm did bring another .9 inches of rain to an already-saturated Pipestone.

Thunderstorms rolled into the city again the night of June 15. The storms left another 1.4 inches of rain. Added to the rain that fell on June 12 and 13, more than two inches of rain were added to June's record. It continued to rain throughout most of the next week, causing the judicial drainage ditch to again rise to dangerous levels. Fortunately, the water that inundated the city quickly receded.

Pipestone was under another flood advisory on Tuesday, June 29. Three inches of rain fell that afternoon. This time, however, the waters crested before they hit large portions of northeast Pipestone. Dean Williams, former Pipestone Soil and Water Conservation District manager, said that floodwaters crested around midnight. The water level was two feet below the May 7–8 flood stage. Damage to property was reported, sewage seeped into basements, and some fields were flooded. The rainfall, one of the largest reported in the county, fell in just over an hour, flooding many of the same city streets that had been flooded on May 7. The ground was still saturated from the heavy rains of the past six weeks.

Many volunteers turned out on the afternoon of June 29 to help fill and distribute sandbags. At 6:30 P.M., the street flooding had subsided, but water in the judicial ditch continued to rise. The floodwaters crested at 10 P.M., but more rain was expected throughout the night.

For the second time that week, volunteers reported for sandbagging duty the night of July 3. Rain had been falling continuously for five days. A three-inch rain that fell on Tuesday had created an emergency: water was escaping the banks of the judicial ditch. City employees and volunteers attempted to slow flooding in the ditch. The emergency was barely over when it began to rain again. A light rain fell on Wednesday (.02 inches, along with hail) but on Thursday heavy rain fell in some areas. Over 1.5 inches of precipitation fell Saturday morning, creating another potential disaster. It rained steadily for over four hours, from 10 P.M. to 2 A.M., adding another inch to the rising total.

Floodwaters rose steadily until midnight. Many homes and businesses were flooded again. Tianna Trailer Park was flooded with two feet of water, but it did not reach the section where people lived. By 1:30 A.M., the water began to recede.

With its seemingly never-ending cycle of rain and flooding, 1993 was an unusual year. Pipestone's weather-related problems were exacerbated by poor environmental and engineering decisions made almost eighty years earlier in addition to the city's continuing policy to allow building in the floodplain and its fringe.

One City, One Ditch, One Big Problem

Julie Porter

Winnewissa Falls is one of the most splendid sights in southwestern Minnesota. It is the spot where Pipestone Creek cataracts over a red quartzite ledge, within the boundaries of the Pipestone National Monument, on its way to join South Dakota's Big Sioux River. It has always been a sacred place to the Native Americans of the area. Here is the home of the Great Pipestone Quarries, home of the peacepipe.

According to Sioux legend, "The Great Spirit was angered by the warring of its people; so he called all the nations of the earth together. They assembled in the valley of the pipestone. Standing on a pinnacle of rock, he bade them to lay down their arms and live like brothers. As he spoke, water gushed forth from the rocks nearby, forming the falls as it flowed over the precipice." In this legend, the Great Spirit used the creation of the falls to instill peace among people. It seems ironic that these same falls have been surrounded by controversy for almost a century.

In 1916 a plan to dramatically alter the red quartzite ledge led to the beginning of the enduring controversy. The rim of the falls lay higher than the land directly upstream, creating Pipestone Lake, a natural holding place for excess water in wet years. From the lake, the water dropped more than 25 feet from the ledge to run on and widen again into Duck, Crooked, and Whitehead lakes downstream. Hearings to establish a judicial ditch in Pipestone County were supported by the Pipestone Indian School, a federally funded facility designed to teach farming techniques to Native American students. The plan for the creation of the ditch, to be partially located on the school's land, included blasting a deep channel up to the ledge, thereby draining Pipestone Lake. This would create 18 additional acres for the school to use for growing crops and raising livestock. In its effort to be more self-supporting, the school would be less reliant on the federal government for funding.

When hearings for the establishment of the ditch began, area farmers protested and vowed to take their case to the Supreme Court. However, the local courts ruled in favor of the ditch. An appropriation of $3,500 was obtained and approximately four feet of jasper rock were blasted away to lower the rim of the falls by seven feet. The ditch, the only one to be built in Pipestone County, became known as Judicial Ditch No. 1. After lowering the falls, a deep channel was dynamited behind the falls upstream and the stone rubble was piled high along the banks. The channel took over a portion of Pipestone Creek and eventually stretched 14 miles northeast, thereby altering a portion of watershed at the height of the Coteau des Prairies' western slope. The project cost reached $61,000, which was assessed to the farmers on both sides of the ditch. (Because a judicial ditch was built and repaired under the jurisdiction of the district courts, the people who benefitted most by its construction were assessed the cost.) Along with the construction of the ditch, over 60 miles of drainage tile were laid to flow into it.

In later years, farmers took advantage of the steeper stream gradient of Pipestone Creek and straightened the channel of the creek throughout most of its length, in effect creating another ditch whose water flowed towards the falls with greater velocity. Efficient drainage upstream, coupled with the loss of Pipestone Lake's capacity as a holding area, sent excess water into areas which, at the time, were sparsely populated. Over the years, the city of Pipestone expanded into those areas which were at risk for inundation.

Many of Pipestone's residents, like Helena Carlson, owner of the Arrow Motel and Fort Pipestone (both of which were flooded in 1993), believed that the ditch caused the flooding in the northern part of Pipestone. She was particularly upset, because the ditch is not a natural waterway. Others blame the falls itself, claiming that the water cannot get over fast enough and backs up as if behind a dam.

Various solutions have been proposed to mitigate the problem. One suggestion is the construction of a diversion channel near the Pipestone National Monument to allow excess water to flow around the falls and the city. This plan would require a five-year environmental impact study, a great deal of money, and the agreement of the National Park Service. Another plan suggests simply building higher banks along critical areas of the ditch. Doug Haeden, Pipestone County highway engineer, argues that the county should retain the excess floodwater upstream in the rural areas before slowly releasing it through a dike and into the city. To date, no solutions have been acted upon. Many residents of Pipestone are angry that when heavy rains fall, the water rushes into the city.

Native Americans came to the Pipestone quarries believing this area to be sacred. The Great Spirit had created peace among the native tribes. The dynamiting of Winnewissa Falls and the creation of the ditches not only transformed the aesthetics of this sacred place, it also shattered a centuries-old peace. The environmental impact of these actions has stirred up conflict between the residents of Pipestone and the government which has lasted for many generations.

Winnewissa Falls prior to 1917

–Minnesota Historical Society, from *Pipestone Reservation Park: A Development of Pipestone Indian Reservation,* by Ralph J. Boomer, pg. 1A

Winnewissa Falls one year after the flood of 1993

–Julie Porter

Three Crests of the Des Moines

Janet Timmerman

Hard rains on top of saturated soil were the chief cause of flooding in southwestern Minnesota during the wet spring of 1993. The spring downpours left the city of Jackson and Jackson County treading water all summer. The city was first mobilized on May 7 and 8 when especially hard rain hit the upper watershed of the Des Moines River. Over 200 volunteers worked seven hours to fill and place sandbags along the river, which runs through the heart of Jackson. City workers, with the permission of the Pollution Control Agency, plugged storm sewers, started sump pumps, and began diverting sewer and storm-sewer water into the river untreated.

Problems upstream made the situation worse. Worthington, a town of 10,000 west of Jackson, regularly dumps surface water runoff into the Heron Lake watershed that, in turn, runs into the Des Moines. An estimated 50 million gallons of additional water from Worthington went into the Des Moines and through Jackson. The river crested at 16 feet, 4 feet above flood stage, but the sandbag levee held. Jackson County applied for Federal Disaster Assistance, sandbags were taken away, and Jackson got back to the business of everyday life.

On June 17, 10 inches of rain fell in the Lake Shetek area, the Des Moines River's headwaters. Volunteers in Jackson again came out to fill sandbags. This time things went more smoothly due to previous practice. This time the river crested at 16.34 feet, but again the sandbags held and the river went on by. This time sandbags were left in place. They were in place when, after another downpour upriver, the Des Moines crested at 16.48 feet on July 6. The greatest worry was keeping the sewers from backing up, but the pumps kept going and damage was minimized.

Meanwhile, the county had heard nothing about being offered disaster aid. Finally on July 15, the Federal Emergency Management Agency added Jackson County to its roster of deserving counties, two months after its first application. No more crests came down the Des Moines that summer. Area farmers threw in the towel and gave up trying to grow a crop. Many signed up for the 0/92 program and simply disced under their half-grown fields.

The city of Jackson faced the high cost of diverting the floods from its doorstep. That cost ran as high as $108,000—part of the cost of being a river town during wet times.

Yogi Bear kept on smiling, though water rose to his chin in the Ashley Park playground
–Jackson County Pilot

"Whiskey's for Drink'n and Water's for Fighting" _____

Janet Liebl

For those who farm the 850 acres flooded for the last two out of three years, Mark Twain's lines ring true: "Whisney's for drink'n and water's for fighting." In this case fighting about how much and how fast the water should flow through a four-mile stretch of land. The controversy is not a new one, it has been going since the founding of the Lac Qui Parle-Yellow Bank Watershed District in the early 1970s. It is a fight over who would benefit from levee and floodway channels and who would suffer. This situation leads to the question, who and in what degree do those involved benefit or suffer and who decides.

In the spring of 1994 two government agencies went to battle on these questions. The Army Corps of Engineers along with the board of the Lac Qui Parle-Yellow Bank Watershed District proposed one levee and a series of four floodway channels along the Lac Qui Parle to help hasten the speed of the water flowing through this stretch. Floodway channels would be built to allow some of the excess water to flow in a more direct path to the Minnesota River and this would alleviate some of the pressure caused by backed up water at flood stage and allow water to flow through the natural channel when the river is at normal levels. Opposition developed from those who lived downstream, as well as from the DNR and a Montevideo group, "Clean Up Our River Environment," or CURE. Opponents feared that this project would only increase flooding somewhere else, increase the influx of sediment, and harm some species of fish that live in the river.

Administrative law judge Allen Klein recommended the DNR deny the permits needed to start construction of the project called Lac Qui Parle River Floodways. DNR Commissioner Rod Sando agreed with this recommendation and concluded that the project would only increase pollution of the Lac Qui Parle River and affect the Minnesota River as well. He also said it would harm important fish habitats.

The Lac Qui Parle-Yellow Bank Board has worked 10 years to achieve the permits and spent thousands of dollars in attorney fees. When the project was denied, the board's attorney, Kevin Stroup, appealed the matter; at this time the project is still in the court system. In proposing the project the board had a study done by the Soil Conservation Service that concluded that the work would only increase the flow of water downstream from the spillways by three hours at a depth of less than two inches. They felt this met one objection to the proposal which was to do a minimum of damage to land downstream. The floodway channels and levee were developed to assist in a five-year flood. The SCS person who did the study assured the board this project would help to control damage in that area for all floods.

The DNR and others opposed to the project were pleased with the decision. They felt the SCS study did not represent the full spectrum of the people and environment affected. CURE hoped this decision would change the way floodplain management strategies are developed and that farmers and others would seek out alternative ways to manage floodplains and rivers. Two alternatives have been suggested.

One would be to plant flood-resistant grasses for grazing instead of planting crops. The second would be to place the land in the program known as RIM or Reinvest in Minnesota. Both alternatives are unsatisfactory to the landowners directly affected by the project. Some acreage is under water some of the time in most recent years so there would be no place to move the livestock during this time. They opposed the RIM alternative more vociferously. If a farmer allows his land to go into the RIM project, the farmer gives a permanent easement to the DNR for his land in exchange for a one-time payment for the land at the current land price. The farmer does not give up ownership of the land and therefore must pay taxes each year on the land that yields no annual income and is of no use to him.

This controversy, still unresolved, is an example of how water—particularly when it comes in great floods—divides people along lines of interest, occupation, and location.

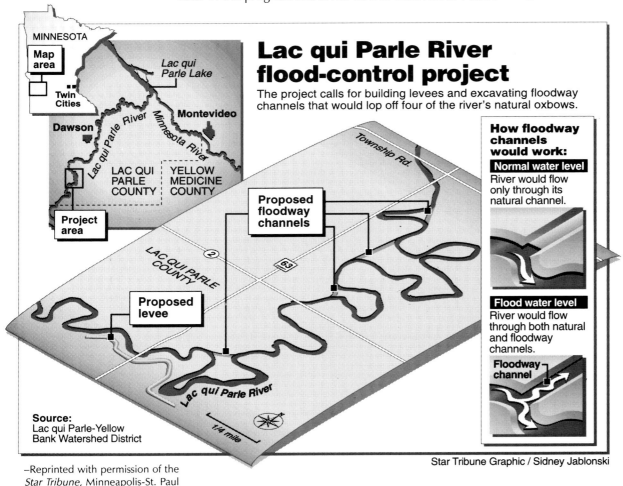

Lac qui Parle River flood-control project

The project calls for building levees and excavating floodway channels that would lop off four of the river's natural oxbows.

MINNESOTA
Map area
Twin Cities

Lac qui Parle Lake
Lac qui Parle River
Montevideo
Dawson
Minnesota River

LAC QUI PARLE COUNTY | YELLOW MEDICINE COUNTY

Project area

Proposed floodway channels

Township Rd.

LAC QUI PARLE COUNTY

Proposed levee

Lac qui Parle River

1/4 mile

How floodway channels would work:

Normal water level
River would flow only through its natural channel.

Flood water level
River would flow through both natural and floodway channels.

Floodway channel

Source:
Lac qui Parle-Yellow Bank Watershed District

Star Tribune Graphic / Sidney Jablonski

–Reprinted with permission of the
Star Tribune, Minneapolis-St. Paul

Septic Tanks and Sump Pumps and the King of Rock and Roll

Howard Mohr

During the biblical rains and floods of 1993, we lived in Lucas Township, Section 33, Lyon County, where there's no lake, no creek, no major county ditch, no Wal-Mart, no sidewalks, no municipal sewage plant, no storm sewer. This was all to our advantage. We watched our neighbors try to farm around the new ponds in their fields, watched them eventually harvest a miserable crop. We sympathized with our friends and fellow human beings in Marshall and points south. It was a cool, damp summer right in the middle of Global Warming. My uncle Tom said he thought we were having Global Cooling and that in his opinion we weren't driving our cars nearly enough.

Eventually the water caught up with us. Our septic tank (the main part of the simple, efficient, gravity-flow waste-processing system used exclusively in rural areas) backed up when the drain field became inundated by groundwater that had reached the surface in many places. We were living on an underground lake, I suppose, but there weren't any walleyes in it. The effluent from the septic tank and groundwater wanted to flow into the house now. In addition, the drainage system around the house, meant to keep the foundation and basement dry, filled up and flowed with groundwater at a rate barely below the GPM (Gallons Per Minute, for the uninitiated) of the sump pump in the sump pit. It was war, or at least a police action.

It was also a practical learning experience. There was no way to keep from learning. It was hands-on experience and also hands in, feet in, and a couple of times when I slipped, butt and back in, experience. If you are interested, I am now an authority on hose couplers, sump pumps, transfer pumps, connectors, hydrology, sewage, two-inch drain plugs, one-way valves, and wrong-size spark plugs in transfer pump gasoline engines that make them hard to start in the dark in the pouring rain and lightning as the water gets closer and closer to the stuff in the paper boxes in the basement that you think is priceless just because you've had it stored for 30 years.

After our sewer system flooded and I plugged the basement drain somewhat successfully, we showered outdoors, using water in a hundred feet of solar-heated garden hose on those rare days when the sun came out, or we carried hot water outside to bathe. We washed clothes in the automatic washer by extending the drain hose through a window into the grove of trees via piggy-backed lengths of sump pump hose. We wore the same clothes longer. We slowly took on a pioneer-style hardy seediness of mind and body.

We used the outhouse for eight weeks. The flush toilets just sat there in our house: Archaeological wonders, clean white sculpture that even Jesse Helms could admire if not fund. But that lovely little shack two-and-a-half shoulder-widths wide was high and dry the whole summer. By early September, there was a beaten path between it and our house.

Our outhouse was grandfathered in when we bought our five acres in 1970. It had served two generations of families at least. It had been moved several times during its peak years, for reasons that should be clear to even city dwellers. It is constructed of scrap lumber, but it is solid and I have always kept it somewhat shingled and fairly level (to control user vertigo) over the years. In fact, in 1991 (Or was it 1989? Does it matter?), I converted it from a two-seater to a one-seater and painted the interior white. I even fixed the door latch so you didn't have to hold the door with your knee to keep it from flopping open. If you didn't want it open.

But the outhouse was mostly rustic decoration until the summer of '93, although visitors from the cities would occasionally utilize it (or pretend to utilize it, perhaps—I did not investigate) for nostalgic purposes, but did voice fears of plunging through the spongy floor. There's nothing but the ground three inches under the floor. The dug hole is located immediately below the seat. The greatest fear for our civilized visitors seemed to be the possibility of small mammals waiting in the pit for the right prey. Sure, groundhogs have been known to dig under outhouses into the pits, but they are vegetarians.

The big surprise for me—I don't speak for the whole family in this matter—was that after six weeks of living in backwaters, I expected to have developed an evangelistic appreciation of modern conveniences. I could hear myself telling the reporter, "Boy, I'll never take indoor plumbing for granted again." But nobody covered our story. My mother, of course, was very interested on a daily basis, sometimes calling twice a day from St. Paul. But an odd thing happened. Well, more than one odd thing, but this odd thing was that I began to like the outhouse. Preferred it. It was functional low-tech at its most admirable. Decades rolled back during that stroll to the mini-cathedral out by the chicken shed. You could hear the birds singing while you meditated. My only regret was that the Sears Catalogue had become extinct and was not available for its intended use.

And as for carrying out the handwashing and teeth-brushing water in the five-gallon pail we kept under the faucet in the utility sink—no problem. It was exercise and we certainly used a lot less water out of our well with that system. I got to feeling I would just go with the flow and move farther and farther away from indoor plumbing. Eventually I would sell the stove and the refrigerator in the *HyVee Trader*. I would cast the lines free and sail away. Wear the

–Sketch by Julie Porter

same clothes for weeks, months. Stop all subscriptions. Tap the screen of the TV set with a hammer and commit it to the earth. Stop listening to the radio so much. Make salads out of native grasses and plants. Take up the accordion.

I was eventually overruled in my dream of the simple life by a two-thirds majority of the family, who had heard this back-to-the-land-escape-from-civilization speech many times before, usually after I had passed my half-hour threshold in a shopping mall.

Another odd thing was that I began to look on the bright side of a backed-up septic tank and a basement on the verge of flooding cataclysmically if the electricity to the pumps stopped. My hat was off to the Minnesota Valley Rural Electric Co-op. The lights blinked a couple of times, but that was all. So I toted up the positives, eschewing the negatives. I had, for example, learned everything there is to know about septic tanks: design, installation, physics and chemistry of, deficiencies. I became one with my septic tank. I wrote two chapters of what I thought might be my next book, *Zen and the Art of Septic Tanks.* I liked what I finished, but I wasn't confident that a New York publisher would think it was the next *Bridges of Madison County.*

And then it happened. On July 3 at 2:45 A.M. to be precise. It was the very day 35 years earlier that Jody and I had our first date. We celebrate that beginning more than our wedding anniversary. It had been raining cats and dogs for hours and I had been waking in the basement from troubled sleep to my alarm every half hour since the ten o'clock

news to check the sump pump that was running continuously to the max. As I passed by the open door to the furnace room on my way to the sump pit, I saw Elvis over in the corner by my glove supply and extension cords, sitting on one of our U.S. Government surplus folding chairs, noodling on his guitar. It was the Elvis before all his troubles, confident and trim. He looked straight at me, winked, pointed his finger and said "Keep rockin' Babe." And then he was gone. I forgot to say that Elvis was wearing five-buckle overshoes.

Throughout the summer there was only one more low ("Let's wire the place with dynamite and go to the desert."), several highs ("Boy, these two-inch, three-horse transfer pumps will do 12,000 gallons an hour, believe it or not—a great machine."), and a minor epiphany that involved my flash of insight into the cosmic connection between food and waste.

But that's not to say I want the flooding to happen again. I've got all the good out of it I can.

Anxious Days and Nights

David Pichaske

In the spring and summer of 1993, the sump pump ran from mid-May through the end of August. Somewhere in the middle of the summer it was joined by a second pump, which Michelle and I had to buy in Minneapolis, local suppliers having sold out. So two pumps worked continuously, day after day, week after week, all summer long. Periodically we peered into the basement to watch the floodwater ooze through the cinderblocks in the basement walls, pour in small rivulets down the wall, and empty into the pool that covered the floor.

As long as the water's depth held between the second or third step, the well pump, iron filter, and water softener were safe; the electrical connections on all three were four feet off the floor. Two pumps, working continuously, kept the water level steady.

The well water was, of course, all contaminated; we drank bottled water and canned juices. I showered at school. Mildew was another problem with all the heat and humidity. So, too, were mosquitoes.

Our biggest worry, however, was the rain, and the level of the river itself, which flooded the lower reaches of the back yard higher than any spring I could remember. It closed in on the oak seedling, to its roots, half way up the stem, to the leaves, and over, so I lost it somewhere beneath the brown soup. Away from the river, small pools formed in depressions, threatening what remained of the garden. The brown water crept toward the rhubarb and the garage.

Using a carpenter's balance, I sighted a level line from the top of a maple stump beside the garage to a tree down by the river. It struck the trunk 3½ feet above the water. The top of my stump was 2 feet, 3 inches from the ground. A rise of 15 inches would bring the river to the base of the stump. A few inches more would lift it over the cement lip of the back stairs to the basement, although by then it would probably be flooding in that hole dug by the squirrel or gopher or woodchuck or whatever it was that had burrowed into the basement.

A level line sighted from stump to house hit the wall just about a foot up. A rise of 24 inches would bring the Minnesota to my doorstep. When we weren't reading news stories, listening to weather forecasts, or checking pumps and river, Michelle and I drove to town to watch the cataracts of brown floodwater pulsing over the Granite Falls dam, watching limbs, logs, whole trees pile up behind the dam's wooden superstructure. (Beams slid into the grooves of steel I-beams embedded in the concrete added an additional three feet to the dam's height.) We watched water behind the dam creep toward the VFW, and the water below the dam creep toward the back door of Ladner's Hardware.

Briefly, I considered laying in supplies of sand and sandbags, or just digging a small levee around the riverside edge of the house. But I didn't.

One night we received a call from the sheriff's office, a public courtesy call announcing the possibility that debris might shatter the dam's wooden superstructure. Nothing definite, merely a possibility. If the timbers went, areas downriver could expect a three-foot rise in the river level. Nobody was being urged to evacuate just yet; this was merely a public service call.

Mentally I did the math; 15 inches to the stump, a few more inches into the basement. Basement gone for sure, along with all the electrical connections there. Another foot and a half? Probably the porch floor, maybe the living room and kitchen floor as well. The rugs. The lower levels of the book shelves. The furniture. The pool table. The hardwood floor. All those boxes of Spoon River Poetry Press books. Probably $30,000 worth of books. I didn't even want to think about securing all that stuff. I certainly didn't want to imagine my loss if I didn't secure it.

Those were anxious days and nights. If the dam did go, what kind of warning would we get . . . if we got any warning at all? Should we go in to work? Should we sit at home? Should we watch by the dam? How abrupt would the break be? How long would it take that pulse of water to cover the three miles from town to our place? Would a drop of three feet of water backed up behind the dam really translate to an increase of three feet of water spread out across the valley in our neighborhood? Where was that flood insurance policy, anyway?

And what could we possibly do? If the rain stopped, the river would drop. That's the way it worked. Simple. Everyone knew that.

In my muddle, I did nothing except move the car and truck to the far end of the drive, up by the road. No sandbags. No levee. No sustained watch by river or dam. Just a lot of fretting and telephone talk and monitoring of pumps and water levels and weather reports.

The dam did not burst. The river subsided of its own volition. The level of basement water dropped to the first step, then below the step, finally into the sump hole. We pulled the second pump. The first settled into intermittent service. Summer melted to fall, which brought troubles of its own.

The 1993 flood story proved to be anxiety, but not disaster. A kind of anticlimax. That was okay by me.

Under Siege: Flooding in the State Parks

Rebecca Schlorf

Damage from the floods of 1993 affected many travelers, hikers, and campers, both those from Minnesota and those from neighboring states. The floods made no exception for state property. State parks in the southwestern Minnesota region were heavily damaged. Vegetation was watered down, thrown together, and ripped apart like a tossed salad. Camden State Park southwest of Marshall was closed for five days to repair a collapsed section of railroad track running through the park. The dam in Split Rock Creek State Park near Pipestone burst in the May 8 flood. Lac Qui Parle State Park's campground became a floodplain.

Not only did Camden State Park have the holiday floods to contend with, but two more floods as well. Flooding began with the spring snow melt at the end of March. The river reached heights not seen in five years. The other flood occurred August 14 and 15 with 3.9 inches of rain during another one of the park's high attendance times, the Camden Wildlife Art Exhibit. Between May and August of that year, Camden received 26.13 inches of rain, twice the normal amount. The park was completely or partially closed for 16 non-successive days. Over a fifth of the park's average annual income was lost due to a 32 percent decline in the number of campers and a 22 percent decline in overall attendance.

Railroad tracks in Camden State Park

–Debbie Myrvik, DNR

The damage to Camden included many landslides along the banks of the Redwood River. Saturated soil along the banks gave way. Plant roots were not strong enough to hold the soil in place. Sediment and trees were washed away into the river, causing blockage and further problems downstream. Slides occurred all along the banks of the Redwood, but the biggest slide occurred minutes before a Burlington Northern train came through the park. Luckily the railroad was checking tracks before trains passed through and found the collapsed section in time. The track, frequently used to haul coal, had to be quickly repaired. The park closed for five days to allow repair crews to do their work. When the track was rebuilt, tile drains were installed to allow easy drainage and to prevent future track damage. This slide, like many others that occurred in Camden, affected about forty feet of the steep river bank.

Bridges crossing the Redwood River in Camden Park were the biggest problem. The bridge in the north end of the park at the old entrance from Lynd was knocked out in the May 8 flood by a large cottonwood tree that became lodged beneath the bridge. As the water rose, the tree acted as a lever lifting the bridge and throwing it into the river, which carried it about a quarter of a mile downriver. The road coming from another bridge in the park was washed out on one side, making travel to the northern section of the park impossible for a few weeks. A low bridge designed to withstand seasonal flooding was submerged most of the summer and held back much debris.

Some good came of this muddy mess. The flooding sped up projects and maintenance in the park, such as the installation of a footbridge near the swimming beach, the building of which had been indefinitely postponed. The replacing of the bridge at the north end of the park now included the building of the footbridge as well. A boardwalk was installed on one of the highly eroded trails, and other trails were widened. The clean-up took place for months afterward. Community-service sentences by courts provided people to help clean up debris and trails during the summer of 1993, and the Minnesota Conservation Corps spent a good part of the summer of 1994 cleaning up.

At Split Rock Creek State Park, a dam holding the 80-acre Split Rock Lake gave way in the May 8 flood, draining the lake. This had a bad effect on the fishing opener, and for park attendance that summer which was down about 50 percent. The dam, however, was quickly replaced. Plans for a new dam were drawn up and construction was begun in September, funded by the Federal Emergency Management Agency, the Minnesota bonding bill, and the Department of Natural Resources.

The dam was rebuilt with a greater holding capacity. It would hold a flood slightly greater than the 100-year event. The dam was also rebuilt stronger with clay instead of dirt. It had to be built wider as a result of erosion during the flood. A handicap-accessible walkway was installed across the new dam and native prairie grasses were planted nearby. The depth of the lake was increased by removing the lakebed silt, a modification that enhanced fish and plant growth. A pilot project, or kids' crew, was hired to clean up some of the debris.

Other state parks suffered damage as well. Lac Qui Parle State Park was underwater most of the summer. It was closed for about 80 days during the summer. The campground was

flooded and acted as the area floodplain. Trees died because of the excess water, and areas had to be replanted and seeded. Old or damaged trees were replaced, and gravel was added to roads to prevent further flow of water and erosion. Fort Ridgely, Upper Sioux, and Blue Mound state parks also suffered damage.

The restored parks presented some bonuses for visitors and community members. Maintenance projects were taken care of more quickly, improving the quality of the parks. Temporary employment for young adults was created. Although the state parks suffered low attendance and physical harm, in the end they have come out well with new trails and other beneficial structures.

Split Rock Creek Dam damage

–Pipestone County Star

An Island for Livestock

Rebecca Schlorf

Most of the livestock problems in Minnesota in 1993 were indirectly related to the wet weather and flooding. Poor pasture conditions contributed to increased bacterial and viral infections in livestock. Inadequate growing conditions led to poor nutrient levels in feed crops, changing protein, vitamin, and trace mineral levels in livestock. Toxic fungi (mycotoxins) grew in silage causing livestock to refuse feed or become ill, which in turn decreased production. All of these factors contributed to reduced livestock production in 1993.

An immediate effect of the floods on livestock was the disease brought on by wet conditions and the cool tem-

Cows stranded on a new island near Pipestone

–Pipestone County Star

peratures, which lowered their immune systems. Pathogens were more prevalent due to the wet forage conditions, and greater exposure to pathogens led to more bacterial infections. Mastitis, a bacterial infection of the udders, increased among dairy herds. This ailment may have contributed to a decline in milk production. Salmonella, a bacterial infection that can infect many of the major organs in swine, was commonplace. The flooding also caused contamination of water and other environmental conditions that contributed to infections and disease.

Poor feed was due to inadequate growing conditions (high moisture coupled with low temperatures). The Minnesota Extension Service reported milk production down in Minnesota compared to 1992. The cool, wet weather affected the quality of hay and forage which, in turn, affected milk production in the Midwest. However, milk production was not significantly influenced by the effects of the floods.

The cool, wet weather before harvest contributed to ear rot in corn and to scab in wheat, barley, oats, and rye. (These fungi produce mycotoxins.) Elevators sold more mold inhibitor than in previous years, a mixture of vitamins and minerals that combat the growth of toxic fungi in silage. Increased pre-harvest moisture contributed to mycotoxins, one of which is called vomitoxin (or DON), which is especially prevalent in corn. These are harmful mostly to swine, because they weaken their immune systems and and leave the swine vulnerable to other diseases. It also causes swine to refuse the feed, thereby decreasing production. In Au-gust 1994, Stephanie Bethke from the Veterinary Diagnostic Laboratory of Minnesota reported that in feed from the 1993 crop, "normally we find one case a week testing producer feed [for vomitoxins], now we are finding about 67 cases per week."

Livestock owners faired better than crop farmers. The loss of livestock was not as significant as the loss of crops; however, the flooding of 1993 did not make things any easier for livestock. More money than usual had to be spent to keep the livestock healthy and productive in the face of floodwaters and to fight vomitoxins after the waters had receded.

> *"Water has been described as the most important nutrient for swine health, and sometimes diagnosing water and feed problems can be challenging for practitioners."*
> —Swine Practitioners, March 1993

The Losing Hand

Betting on a Crop in 1993

Rebecca Schlorf

Farmers in southwestern Minnesota gambled against the weather throughout 1993. By April, 12.09 inches of rain had fallen in southwestern Minnesota (District 7), whereas during an average year only 8.7 inches are normally received. Already saturated from the previous fall rains and winter runoff, wet soils delayed planting. Anxious farmers hustled to plant their still damp fields, only to encounter the problem of soil compaction under the weight of heavy farm machinery. (Compaction meant poor soil aeration, which, in turn, led to stunted growth and poor root systems.)

By May 8, the "lucky farmers" who had gotten fields planted found their fields drowned by the Mother's Day flood. (Although many factors, such as maturity, species, and weather conditions contribute to how long a crop can withstand sub-

> *"I would say we are fortunate; we only lost twenty percent of our crops, but those closer to the river lost considerably more."*
>
> –James Fuhrmann

mersion, corn can usually withstand two days under water, and soybeans only slightly more.) When crops did succumb, farmers scrambled to local seed stores to purchase more seed. So began the game of switching crops and switching from full-season varieties to late-season varieties of soybeans.

As many farmers began replanting, they were greeted by the Father's Day flood on June 17. If their fields were not under water, farmers could still stay in the game with late season soybean varieties that could be planted as late as July 15. Their machinery ready and loaded, they set out

Stranded tractor near Redwood Falls

–Redwood Gazette

once more to do their job. Again, some were unsuccessful even in getting their equipment into the field and making use of it there. They ended up surrendering their tractors to the mud. Others took their "last-ditch efforts" to plant water-logged fields to the air. Planting from airplanes cost $10 per acre plus the cost of seed. Even at that, this idea seemed worth the try. Better, they reasoned, to have some crop than no crop at all. If soil and weather were just right, seeds would germinate; however, this desperate, high-risk technique turned out to be unsuccessful.

After the final blow of the July 3 rains, many farmers hoped that some of their crops, if planted, would be salvageable. A few farmers who did not have a crop in the field attempted to plant buckwheat, which grows best in a cold, wet climate. Cool temperatures had been plaguing the area most of the summer and an early frost seemed likely. On October 1, frost struck southwestern Minnesota (two weeks earlier than the average killing frost date) taking away the last hope for mature crops. Farmers had played a losing game to the end.

In the planting season of 1993, poor yields were a result of poorly matured crops and low quality due to the prolonged cool, wet weather and early frost. Corn yields were down in the 10-county southwestern Minnesota area by 52.9 percent and soybeans were down by 47.4 percent from the previous year. Harvested acres were significantly down as well. A good crop in 1993 was not in the cards. The only game left was government aid.

–Minnesota Agricultural Statistics Service 1994

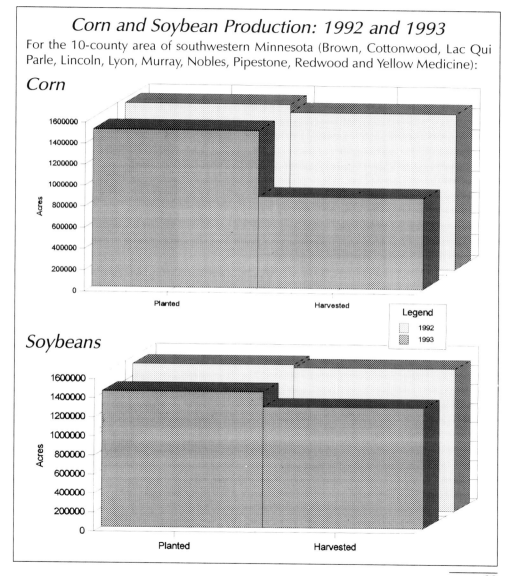

Corn and Soybean Production: 1992 and 1993

For the 10-county area of southwestern Minnesota (Brown, Cottonwood, Lac Qui Parle, Lincoln, Lyon, Murray, Nobles, Pipestone, Redwood and Yellow Medicine):

Paradise Lost

Janet Timmerman

The origins of the 1993 floods in southwestern Minnesota were first sketched in the soil a century ago in the form of straight furrows dug behind bullditchers as they channeled water from a wetland into nearby creeks.

The southwest corner of Minnesota lies within the Prairie Pothole Region, an area once scraped by glaciers and left pitted with wetlands. Even the high land of the Coteau des Prairies is spotted with damp sags and rushy sloughs. Pre-settlement estimates of wetland acreage, based on early surveyor's notes, are sketchy at best. Cumulatively, they suggest that wetlands covered over 900,000 acres in the 10-county area stretching from Lac Qui Parle County to the Iowa border. Fewer than 10 percent of those original wetlands survive to harbor wildlife and impound water.

> *"[Marshes] have their own life-rich genuineness and reflect forces that are much older; much more permanent, and much mightier than man."*
>
> —Paul L. Errington

In an earlier era of inexpensive land and a seemingly endless supply of water, the work done by wetlands was not adequately discerned, nor would it have been deemed important had it been understood. Only after years of thorough and efficient drainage, by means of tiling, ditching, and channelization, the true importance of abundant wetlands began to be appreciated. Once seen as a nuisance by farmers, wetlands were drained with the approval and financial help of the federal government. Across a century of settlement, a very intricate and efficient system of draining water from the land developed, which slowly changed the hydrology of the area. Lyon County with over 7,000 miles of county tile and open ditch, and Redwood County with 511 miles of county ditches and over 11,000 miles of county-owned tile, illustrate the high degree of influence drainage has had on hydrology. (These figures do not include privately owned tile.)

Water runs from the land today at a rate greater than ever before. Wetlands adjacent to streams lowered the flow of upland runoff by absorbing the overflow, thereby reducing flooding downstream. Without wetlands, water flows directly into rivers, turning lakesheds into riversheds. Meandering rivers are forced to take on more water than they are capable of containing, creating wider floodplains and numerous problems downstream. As a result, higher levees and deeper channel diversions must be built.

Hydrologists argue that restoration of the upland sloughs would have had little effect on a once-in-a-century event, such as that of the flood of 1993. Restoration would, however, effect a change on the yearly spring runoffs, possibly up to a 25-year event. It would also cut crop losses on lowland acreage that would be restored to its natural state. The importance of wetlands goes far beyond their capacity to mitigate flooding. They also recharge aquifers, provide crucial wildlife habitats, and filter contaminants from runoff waters. A marsh is like a sponge nature uses to clean up after itself. Draining the wetlands broke the original cycle and worsened the effect of extraordinary events like the 1993 floods.

Saving Wetlands Amidst A Flood

Jim Muchlinski

As the upper Midwest dried out from flooding in the summer of 1993, Minnesota's conservation agencies were working to keep some of its land area wet.

The state's Wetland Conservation Act went from being an idea to becoming a permanent part of land management. Many areas of rural Minnesota had lost vast portions of their wetland acres through the practice of tile drainage into ditch systems. With the drainage came a loss of wildlife habitat, a decline in water availability and, some would say, a greater risk of flood-related damage.

After years of draining wetlands at will, the Wetland act mandated that drained or filled areas be replaced by other wetlands having at least equal value. On agricultural land, the replacement could take place on a one-to-one ratio, but the rate goes up to two-to-one on land that doesn't qualify as farm-related.

The state wetland law inspired uncertainty, even a subtle amount of fear, in many individual counties. Provisions that were developed at the state level required local review of drainage and replacement proposals, with the option of appealing to a state board. For county officials, the prospect included a possibility of having to administer an extra program without any extra funding. "Counties need to receive funding or have greater flexibility in implementing the act," said former Yellow Medicine County Environmental Officer Paula Botsford, during a December 1992 public hearing on the Wetland Conservation Act organized by the Minnesota Board of Water and Soil Resources.

Area farmers added their testimony to that of local conservation staff. A particular concern in the minds of many landowners was how the new rules would affect small, shallow, seasonal wetlands known as "nuisance potholes." In some cases, the potholes stood as obstacles on valuable crop acreage, without having the potential to benefit soil or wildlife.

"More flexibility should be provided for nuisance potholes," testified farmer Merle Rost of rural Ivanhoe. "We should either be allowed to drain them as needed or they should be reduced in value" (for tax purposes).

Public forums were held in Marshall and a series of other locations. They led to changes in the program during 1993. Among other things, the start-up of a permanent set of wetland rules was delayed from July 1, 1993, until January 1, 1994, a move that gave local governments more time to decide how to work with the provisions.

Other major changes included an amendment allowing small percentages of wetlands to be drained for purposes like road construction. A revision of wetland banking provisions, which allowed replacements to be used as credits toward future drainage, provided for the banking of created wetlands in addition to those that were restored.

"Ideas from the testimony carried over into legislative session," said state Board of Water and Soil Resources wetlands administrator Greg Larson, in a *Marshall Independent* article published in July 1993. "The changes haven't weakened the act, but they've given local officials greater flexibility."

As the 1993 floods became a memory, the Wetland Conservation Act saw its first test cases. The rules appeared to be having the biggest impact on development within cities, as shown by wetland studies in Tyler and Marshall. Local technical review panels, three-member boards appointed at the county level, had the chance to apply state guidelines within a local framework.

"The technical review panel is there as an option whenever it's needed," said Lyon County Soil and Water Conservation District staff member Rose Anderson, in the July article. "It's a way of making sure that the laws are being followed and that individuals receive fair treatment."

As floodwaters engulfed much of rural Minnesota, the Wetland Conservation Act quietly became a new component of water and natural resources management. Like the flood, itself, it became a source of questions and passions about the future of the region's waters.

Wetland Loss

County	Total Land Acres	Pre-settlement Wetland Acres	Current Wetland Acres
Brown	396,200	196,000	2,000
Cottonwood	416,800	40,000	0
Lac Qui Parle	502,800	172,000	2,000
Lincoln	350,200	40,000	2,000
Lyon	459,000	107,000	1,000
Murray	451,000	33,000	1,000
Nobles	461,200	137,000	less than 1,000
Pipestone	295,100	17,000	0
Redwood	570,600	171,000	1,000
Rock	310,100	3,000	0
Yellow Medicine	493,000	133,000	less than 1,000
Total	4,706,000	1,049,000	approx. 10,000

–Statistics from Jeffrey P. Anderson and William J. Craig,
Growing Energy Crops on Minnesota's Wetlands
(Minneapolis: University of Minnesota, 1984)

Time and Time Again

Julie Porter

The spring of 1993 was not the first time the city of Marshall had to deal with devastating floods. Flooding occurs in Marshall because the Redwood River falls 635 feet on its 40-mile course from Pipestone to Marshall. In addition to this, 10 counties send water into the Redwood River before it reaches Marshall. After the river leaves Marshall, it falls only 38 feet on its 38-mile trip to Redwood Falls. Major floods occurred in Marshall in 1881, 1923, 1957, and 1969.

The winter of 1880–81 was harsh. Over four feet of snow fell in southwestern Minnesota, creating snowbanks up to 20 feet high. On April 20 the melting snows began to flood the lowlands. The Redwood River reached flood stage on April 24. Torrents of water from the melting snow overflowed the banks of the rivers and carried away bridge and railroad tracks. People traveled Marshall's streets in boats. Some people took trips by boat over the flooded prairie from Marshall to places on the Minnesota River. Damage in Marshall was estimated at $5,000. The waters began to recede the next day.

The flood of 1923 was caused by huge bodies of ice that obstructed the river channel. The river had been swollen for a week, but it gave no indication it would overflow its banks. The first break came north of the railroad bridge. Water rose at the rate of 2.5 feet per hour. The water then began to flow onto south Second Street, covering between 15 and 20 acres of adjacent pastureland. By 6:00 P.M., several square blocks between the bridges on Main Street and north Fourth Street were inundated. Nearly 50 houses were surrounded by water in the area of town that was hardest hit. This area stretched from Liberty Park to the north Fourth Street bridge and beyond.

By the following afternoon, the river began to rise again and passed the highest previous mark by 10 inches. There were ice jams at four or five places along the river's course that held back the floodwaters. City workers attempted to open the channel, while hundreds of people gathered along the river to watch the flood spread despite the workers' efforts to dynamite the ice jams. The Redwood subsided nearly as fast as it had risen. With the temperature below the freezing point, the only indication that there had been a flood was the occasional cake of ice lying on the ground the next morning.

The flood of June 1957 inundated 88 percent of Marshall. On June 16, 8 inches of rain fell. On June 21, 3.52 inches of rain fell, making a total of 14 inches for the month. The flood of 1957 was Lyon County's worst flood up to that time. This flood was different from most of the other floods that took place in Marshall. Instead of being caused by melting snow or ice jams, the 1957 flood was caused by heavy rains. Roads were washed out and remained impassable for weeks. Some washed-out bridges were not replaced until the following year.

Residents on the east side of Marshall suffered the least amount of damage, while residents who lived on the south side suffered the most. There was little structural damage

> *"I'll never fall asleep to the sound of falling rain again."*
> —Donata DeBruyckere

*Main Street Marshall
flooding in 1957*

    –Lyon County
    Historical Society

to buildings, but many houses and businesses had to be cleaned up. There were several inches of muck and a foot of sewer water in some houses. The damage to the tri-county area of Lincoln, Lyon, and Redwood counties amounted to $15 million.

In an effort to prevent a disaster like the flood of 1957 from ever happening to the city of Marshall again, the city and county governments, together with the United States Army Corps of Engineers, constructed a 2.5-mile diversion channel at the cost of $2,252,000; $350,000 was spent to acquire land and to build bridges. This diversion channel plan was accepted by the City of Marshall on Dec. 6, 1963.

During the winter of 1968–69 over 82 inches of snow fell. After the snow came the floods. Damage to county roads alone amounted to over $300,000. The damage would have been more extensive had it not been for the newly-created diversion channel. In turn, it was the diversion channel that again saved Marshall from widespread damage during the 1993 floods. And the 1993 floods convinced Marshall of the need to complete the diversion channel, even if it means more water for the farms to the north and east of Marshall.

The 1957 Flood

Joseph Amato

The flood of June 1957 is the one Marshall can't forget. Marshall made the national news with this flood, which was called "The Great Father's Day Flood" and "The Big Rain."

The 1957 flood was caused by rains averaging 5 to 8 inches in the Redwood and Yellow Medicine watersheds and exceeding 10 inches in some places in the Redwood River Valley. Farms lost 10 to 40 tons of soil per acre.

With no diversion channel to deflect the waters descending from the Buffalo Ridge, as occurred in the 1969 flood (an immense spring snow run-off flood) and the 1993 floods, Marshall was inundated by water. With 88 percent of the surface of Marshall covered by water, the city became a shallow lake, traversed by motor boats for four days, until the waters subsided.

> *"Trouble arrives on horseback and departs on foot."*
> –Anonymous

Marshall was literally cut off from the world around it. There are countless stories about people trying to get in or out of Marshall. One woman related the story of a perfectly enjoyable evening on her double date at the drive-in movie the night the rains came. On returning to Ghent, she was confronted by irate parents, who were more disturbed by the rising water than her long hours at the drive-in.

In an essay titled "Troublesome Waters," Todd Synder described how the flood invaded the entire downtown area. A hardware merchant saw fish swimming in the front door of his store and out the back door. A grocer cleaned and sold his label-less cans at a great discount to the public. Joe Louwagie remembered that for months after the flood, supper became a potluck because no one knew what they would get when the family's unmarked vegetable cans were opened.

Disease became a major problem. Typhoid and cholera germs lurked in the standing waters and debris that covered the town and in the sewage that filled buildings and houses. Children at play became children in danger.

Disease was a problem on the farm as well. Farm animals suffered blackleg disease which led to acute lameness and fever. Left untreated, death occurred within 48 hours. Other diseases from wet and moldy feed also affected livestock.

Effective methods of cleaning up flood damage were not generally available, which meant that the flood, like other bad things in life, arrived on horseback and departed on foot.

–Lyon County Historical Society

Photos from the 1957 flood

–Lyon County Historical Society

The 1993 Floods from Four Vantage Points

Jim Muchlinski

Like many residents on Westwood Drive in Marshall, Charles Richeson was grateful for the city's earthen flood control levee.

Richeson told the *Marshall Independent* in August 1993 that six feet of water filled his basement during the Mother's Day flood. Because the basement contained furnishings and hobby equipment, he lost an estimated $20,000 to $25,000 above the insurance coverage.

After the levee was built across Lyon County Road 7 from the Westwood neighborhood, he reported that there were no further problems with flooding in his neighborhood.

"Had the levee been in there at the beginning, I'm sure we wouldn't have had any trouble with the Mother's Day flood," Richeson said.

The issue of the earthen levee extended beyond the Marshall city limits, however. It was regarded as a factor in channeling water from the Redwood River basin into the Cottonwood River basin, which lies south of Marshall over Highway 23.

In the same August article, Dennis Oeltjenbruns said that the levee may have worsened conditions on his land seven miles southeast of Marshall in the Cottonwood basin. More than 100 acres of his crops were drowned out, while soil was badly eroded in places.

As to the idea of making the levee a permanent structure, Oeltjenbruns said, "We will pursue legal action. We won't stand for it."

The levee was later taken down voluntarily, but other flood-control issues remained unresolved, even during the improved weather conditions and bumper crops of 1994.

Upstream from Marshall in the Redwood watershed, a group of Balaton-area landowners opposed an attempt to establish a flood-control dam with a pooling area of about 1,400 acres. The land includes about 100 acres that have been farmed by Marvin Green's family for the past 120 years.

> *"It isn't always where you get the most rain that you get the most water."*
>
> –Tony DeZeeuw

"Marshall is trying to dump their troubles on us," Green said in a February 1994 news article in the *Independent*. "There is no big city or politicians on our side. We're a bunch of farmers."

Different flood concerns emerged northeast of Marshall, downstream from the city and from possible water retention sites. The Redwood River drops several hundred feet from its source until it reaches Marshall, but then abruptly levels off, which caused water to spill over into fields at the height of the 1993 floods.

"All of the water that comes into Marshall has to go through our culverts," said George Louwagie of rural Green Valley in a July 1993 edition of the *Independent*. "Our drainage system wasn't nearly enough to take care of it this summer. The water has been coming too fast and it needs to be looked at."

Temporary dike being built on County Road 7 on the western edge of Marshall

–Jerry Sowden, *Marshall Independent*

Louwagie and more than twenty other Green Valley area farm residents decided to sponsor a river system study by civil engineer Bruce Kelly of Orono. The research was geared toward looking at problems with area flood control and potential solutions for the future.

In discussing the engineer's study, sponsors emphasized that it was not undertaken to assign blame for the 1993 floods, but to consider ways to make sure it didn't happen again. Residents north and east of Marshall remain actively interested in flood retention, either through the large, controversial dam near Balaton or with some other alternative.

"If the water could be stored and sent in more gradually we might be able to avoid some of the damage," said Dean Louwagie of rural Green Valley in the July 1993 article. "Even slowing it down for a few hours would help."

The Flood Within

Toni Beebout-Bladholm

In the summer of 1993, the flood brought more than just a vast amount of water; to some it brought gallons of sewer water. James Zarzana of Marshall said, "There was a terrible noise coming out of the bathroom, and suddenly it started to shoot out of the toilet." This city's sewer system was unable to handle the enormous amounts of water rushing into its pumping stations. Breaks in sewer lines and unsealed manholes also contributed to the overwhelming of the system.

During the Mother's Day flood, Marshall residents were not adequately warned about the dangers of toilet flushing and using water to cook and bathe. No one realized that the water they used often ended up in their neighbor's basement. During the Father's Day flood, the warning was much more clear. The *Marshall Independent* on June 18, 1993, quoted David Frey, the city's wastewater treatment plant supervisor, as saying, "We realize Mother Nature requires people to use some water during the day. But if people can live with a stinky body for a little while, it helps." Unfortunately many residents ended up having sewer water in their basements. Some residents of Hill Street in Marshall had up to four feet of sewage.

During the summer of 1993, it was impossible to deal with the vast amount of water going to the pumping stations and the treatment plant. The total flow for June 1993 was 112.2 million gallons per day (mgd) compared to 85.2 mgd for June 1994, a difference of 27 mgd. The wastewater treatment plant was unable to deal with the velocity of water in June of 1993.

This pressing problem of sewer water did not end with the floods. Some of the same sewer backup problems occurred a year later on August 10, 1994. The question of what to do about the recurring problem remains. Frey stated that, "It would be impossible to develop a system that could handle such vast amounts." It is difficult to explain this to someone who has been afflicted with flooding disasters two or three times.

Some residents have installed shutoff valves in their homes. These valves are used to protect residents' homes from sewer water. One drawback is that when this valve is in place, no water can be used in the entire house. If water is used, it will end up in the basement. Another drawback is that residents are responsible for turning off the valve. If they are not home, there is no point to having the valve. These valves range in cost from $200 to $700. The cost involved is prohibitive for some families.

> "Maybe people will no longer flush and forget it."
>
> –David Frey

There are also some larger problems with the use of shutoff valves. For one thing, where can the water go if everyone uses their valves? Does the whole town simply erupt like a volcano, carrying with it an unpleasant odor? Frey noted, "Most likely, the water would shoot out manholes." Until steps are taken to ensure the stability of the sewer system, many residents of Marshall will continue to face the threat of disaster.

Bill Turgeon, a Marshall resident, said that in the absence of a system-wide solution to the sewer backup problem in

Homeowners posted signs near their homes to identify damaged property

—Jerry Sowden,
Marshall Independent

Marshall, the installation of shutoff valves is the most practical way for homeowners to deal with the situation. However, he feels that in the long run, a city-wide assessment for revamping the sewer system might prove to be a less costly way to reduce the threat of sewer backup throughout the city.

The wastewater treatment plant took a lot of heat in 1993, and the controversy continues. The City of Marshall has taken steps to put a water management plan into action, but this alone will not address the issue of sewer backup the city faces. Improvements must also be made to the treatment plant. With the two plans working together, there is hope that these problems will be eliminated. It won't be too soon for many residents.

The Disparity of Disaster

Jennifer Mathiason

Lack of power means lack of recognition. It is not surprising, therefore, that most Marshall residents do not pay much attention to Camelot Trailer Park. Unfortunately, it took an especially rare occurrence for the city to relate Camelot with the prestigious Westwood Acres. During the floods of 1993, however, they did precisely that. Both Westwood Acres and Camelot Trailer Park were hit harder by the floodwaters than were any of the other neighborhoods within the city of Marshall. For the first time in history, Westwood and Camelot had something in common: both were struggling with the same affliction—water.

When entering the city of Marshall from the west on Highway 23, the spacious, beautiful homes of Westwood Acres are the first dwellings to be seen in the town. This neighborhood lies on the southwestern edge of Marshall and runs adjacent to a portion of the diversion channel and to County Road 7. When the rain poured down onto Buffalo Ridge in the summer of 1993, the floodwaters flowed east toward Marshall and toward Westwood Acres. The water breached the top of County Road 7 and flowed into the backyards of many Westwood residents.

In the case of Westwood and elsewhere, the Minnesota Department of Natural Resources is charged with the determination of what lands are most likely to be affected by flooding. In its most recent 1979 floodplain map, the DNR delineated three types of zones: Zone A is the 100-year floodplain, which has a one percent chance each year of being inundated; Zone B is a 500-year floodplain; and Zone

C has little or no chance of being overrun with water. Structures are allowed in Zone A only if their lowest living area is constructed one foot above the highest potential flood mark and are required to maintain federally-subsidized flood insurance. Very few homes in Westwood Acres lay within

Zone A, an area which lies mostly undeveloped at this time. Homes constructed near the river after it parts from the diversion channel are considered to be in Zone C and are judged to run little risk of flooding. Relying on this DNR assessment, most Westwood residents assumed they were safe and, thus, were unprepared to deal with not only one flood but three in three months. They learned the hard way

Westwood Acres' backyard during the 1993 flood

—Joe Buysse

that man-made boundaries do little to protect them from the wrath of the river.

Westwood Acres was not entirely spared by the emergency levee constructed along County Road 7. Water was already pouring over the road as the structure was being built during the Mother's Day flood. Some residents of Westwood later complained that if the roadbed had been

Camelot Trailer Park inundated by water

—Jerry Sowden,
Marshall Independent

raised during a recent construction project, water would not have breached the road at all. However, a road retention project cannot be built without consideration of what damage may be incurred elsewhere by its construction. The city also had no jurisdiction over the road, which belongs to Lyon County.

Camelot Trailer Park, located in the northeastern corner of the city of Marshall, was also damaged by the floods of 1993. After causing destruction to many homes on Westwood Drive, the floodwaters naturally followed the Redwood River and the man-made diversion channel, and joined before reaching Camelot Trailer Park. The diversion channel ends before Camelot; therefore, it does little to protect the park. Furthermore, the additional rain which fell directly on Marshall during the Mother's Day flood caused the Redwood River, located just one mile from the mobile home park, to spill over its banks, deluging the park.

Camelot Trailer Park is located within Zone A—a 100-year flood zone. Before its development in the late 1960s, this land was a big swamp. Ditch 62, which runs near the park, also contributed to the flooding. Twenty-six years before, the ditch was intended to act as a catchall to prevent rainwater from entering Camelot Trailer Park. Unfortunately, Ditch 62 had never been cleaned out. Consequently, it was full of debris and unable to gather up the floodwater coming from town. Instead, the water simply rolled over the top of the ditch, stopping only as it became trapped inside Camelot Trailer Park.

Mayor Robert Byrnes explained to the Camelot residents that Ditch 62 had been built as a storm water outlet. It has no more than a five-foot drop from its beginning near Super America to where it discharges north at Highway 23. Unfortunately, it is a flat ditch, and if it had been cleaned out, it would not have done much to prevent water from entering the trailer park. According to Mayor Byrnes, FEMA has made plans to reconstruct Ditch 62 by lowering it six feet at its end and building a large retention pond.

In the aftermath of the flood, there was a diversity of opinion in the two communities. Residents of Westwood Acres felt that the city officials did not do their job of preventing, warning, or helping their neighborhood deal with the flooding during the summer of 1993. Roger and Gail Peavey of Westwood Drive, whose home was inundated by the Mother's Day flood, were irate about the lack of warning. "You can't keep water from coming. The problem I had is that the floodwater took a whole day to get to us and we had no warning," said Gail. Her husband agreed, stating (in the May 10, 1993, issue of the *Marshall Independent*), "We didn't see any official come by. I'm disappointed that as high as the water got, they [city officials] didn't sound the alarm." Jeanne Blomme, a neighbor of the Peaveys, also complained that no officials came by to explain what was happening. Furthermore, when Jeanne, seeing water up to her doorstep, called the Marshall Police Department to ask for help, the police simply stated, according to her, "There's no water in Westwood Acres." This neighborhood discovered the flooding when they stepped outside their homes early Sunday morning. It seemed there was an inadequate forecasting system in this area.

Also, many residents in Camelot Trailer Park were quite critical of the city. It did not protect them from the flood, nor did it alleviate problems created by the flood. A few residents believed that city officials somehow even added to the destruction. Many objected to having their homes shown on the media; however, there was little the city could do to hinder camera crews from entering the flooded area. Outsiders driving 4x4 trucks through the park's water-filled streets caused alleged damage to mobile home skirting. A

Children look on as their home is bombarded by water

—Jerry Sowden,
Marshall Independent

few residents complained that the Marshall Police Department did little to stop outsiders from looking into trailer windows. They feared vandalism, although none was reported.

When asked about accusations made by residents of Camelot Trailer Park, Mayor Byrnes said, "I'm hurt that some people are feeling this way." He said the city did its best to help both Westwood Acres and Camelot Trailer Park equally. Some people in the mobile home park did feel that the city did the best they could under the circumstances. Many in Westwood were also supportive of the city, saying they believed that as well.

Residents of Westwood Acres and Camelot Trailer Park equally praised the help they received from their own communities. "In our neighborhood, I thought the help was just incredible. All you had to do was say you needed something and pretty soon somebody was bringing it," Blomme said of her neighbors. Gail Peavey also felt that, in the face of this devastating natural disaster, "The plus thing was the friends that really cared."

The residents of Camelot Trailer Park also felt a pulling together of neighbors. When the sirens went off the first night of the summer flooding, all residents, including pets, were forced into the park's storm shelter. That night a line was drawn between people of different ethnic groups. However, according to resident Shirleen Schwab, by the second night, "We were starting to mingle; and by the third," she added, "we were all just really good friends." Bev Haynes, also of Camelot Trailer Park, agreed: "The flood got us talking to people we normally wouldn't talk to."

The summer of 1994 brought no serious flooding to the Midwest, nor to Marshall, Minnesota. It seems that in one short year many in the town have forgotten the floods of 1993. Westwood continues to be developed with new homes being built southward, closer and closer to the DNR's 100-year flood zone area. Furthermore, the "Kingdom of Camelot" has once again been forgotten. The streets continue to crumble, making it dangerous to drive through, and mobile home skirting on the trailers is left rotting with water damage. It seems that the only winners in 1993 were the media, who gave the residents of Camelot the recognition that they rarely obtain.

Victims' Voices

Toni Beebout-Bladholm

The 1993 flood affected the people of southwestern Minnesota in a variety of ways. Dr. James Zarzana, a professor at Southwest State University who lives on Hill Street, an area of town that suffered the blows of the 1993 flood not once but twice, said, "The flood took trinkets, not treasures." Not only did he have floodwater to contend with, but sewer water as well. Water is one thing, but sewer water is another story. It is a health risk and much more difficult to clean up than rainwater.

When asked what the most valuable thing he lost was, he replied, "Time." His family was not able to go on their usual vacation to see old friends, who had a terminally ill child. It left the Zarzanas with a feeling of great regret. Not only had their home been violated by the flood, but it had taken away from them less tangible things of great importance. Zarzana lost his slides from England and Ireland along with other valuables that were stored in the basement of his home. What was most distressing were the emotional and financial burdens of the flooding.

Jan Kraft lives near Zarzana. Her frustration with the sewer system was central to her experience. On the eve of the Father's Day flood, her carpenter had just completed repairs from the Mother's Day flood. An hour after the carpenter left, a neighbor called Kraft and said they had trouble and that she had better check her own basement. She instantly went into a state of denial; it was supposed to be over, not starting again. "I just sat in the garage looking through cards that had to be thrown away." She had also saved her son's school papers, a link to the past. Tragically those mementos had to be added to the pile of cards, lost forever.

Gail Peavey expressed frustration in an interview. Her concern was with the lack of warning: "What about the civil defense siren? What about someone going door to door? Someone had to have realized the river was rising."

The Peaveys' ability to cope with the storms is amazing, as one looks at photos, home videos, and newscasts of the storm. They were not devastated once, but twice. Literally everything from their basement was beyond salvaging. The rising water levels took not only their basement, but was dangerously close to flooding the second level of their home as well.

> *"On the philosophical side, always remember that the flood took trinkets, not treasures."*
> –James Zarzana

A year later, the Peaveys were still trying to put their lives back together. Their home was still in disarray. Economic strains put the brakes on many home improvement and repair projects. Peavey reflected on her children's things that were lost. It made her wonder, "What do you save and why if it can be taken from you?" It is a question many people were left with after the devastation.

Peavey's grief was shared by her neighbor Jeanne Blomme. Blomme was also frustrated by the lack of warning. She called the police department to ask them what she should do about the rising water levels on Saturday night. They said, "There isn't any water in Westwood." Early the

Camelot resident is carried through the floodwaters

–Jerry Sowden, *Marshall Independent*

next morning, she called back to ask again what she should do. "Move to higher ground," was their reply. Unfortunately, the water levels had already blocked their driveway, making it impossible to move to higher ground. Fortunately for the Blomme family, they were able to rescue a majority of their possessions from the rising water, such as Rich Blomme's light and music show equipment which was stored in the basement. The Blommes' three children were active participants in this salvage work. "They thought everything was exciting at first, but when more and more water came and more and more work had to be done, the fun faded."

It wasn't only urban dwellers who faced losses. Farm families, after watching their livelihoods submerge, were forced to make hard choices about the various government programs offered as relief. The 0/92 program, introduced to accommodate farmers who had lost crops, required participants to plow under crops in return for a payment per acre.

To the David Zwach family, who farms between Milroy and Tracy, this process seemed wasteful. They could do nothing with the part of the crop that had survived, neither use nor donate it. It simply had to be plowed under along with the damaged portion. David Zwach said, "I wish they would never have had this type of program." To David and his wife, Pat, the dilemma presented much mental anguish. Pat said, "We didn't sleep much trying to make the decision. I just knew I would support whatever he decided to do."

The Zwachs said, "Everyone in town thought that we were doing something very wrong."

The opinions of friends and neighbors often influenced how people responded to the disaster. Dave and Pat agree that the views of community members weighed heavily on their minds. In a sense they were pioneers; no one in their area was keen on what 0/92 had to offer, but they went ahead anyway. People from town even came out to inspect their fields and take samples back to town. By taking a stand against the norm, the Zwachs were able to gain some profits from a losing crop. Going out on a limb was not easy, Dave said. "I went to the ASCS office in the morning and didn't make a decision until nearly three o'clock in the afternoon. I just couldn't decide what to do. There were many people that were in the same situation." David finally decided to enroll a portion of his land into the 0/92 program. "I couldn't get myself to go 100 percent, but as it turns out I should have."

It is one step to enroll, but another to drive out to the field and destroy what you worked so hard to create. Both Dave and Pat remember sitting in the field having coffee and just looking out at what was soon to be destroyed. It was one of the hardest decisions and acts that they had to participate in. They both felt that it was something they would never do again, financial loss or not. "If I had it to do over, I wouldn't do things the same," said Dave.

In all the stories of the flood victims, some things remain constant: denial, pain, and loss. What can be done is to learn from the experience; to find ways to protect our communities, homes, and families. Zarzana said, "Become friends with your neighbors, because you never know when you are going to need their help. We all must learn to protect and help each other."

Circle of Bright Ribbons

Joseph Amato

It was eleven o'clock in the evening. The water was escaping the sump hole. The pump couldn't keep up.

We jammed a tennis ball in the sewer. We started moving books from the bottom shelves of our many cases. We put up the boxes of stuff left by our son, who was overseas, and we moved our daughter's wedding gifts upstairs.

We rolled back the rug in the TV room. We swept and directed water as best we could from the bedroom closet where the sump pump was to the sewer drain in the center of the laundry room.

Falling further and further behind, we stood in deeper and deeper water. At two o'clock in the morning the water reached the motor of the sump pump. It stopped. We surrendered.

We went to bed. Somehow we slept as the water filled our basement. My wife woke me at 5 A.M. She had just heard on the radio that the local hardware store was open and selling sump pumps.

Half afraid I would be electrocuted—a fear I experienced over and over again during the next eight hours as water reached to just below the basement electrical outlets—I entered the water from the second stair of the basement steps. Over a half foot of water filled the entire basement. The motors of the washer, the dryer, the furnace, and the water heater were all under water. The partially-submerged exercise bike looked oddly out of place. Our old, long-play records and my favorite albums by Sun House, who plays Mississippi Delta Blues, were drenched. Around the sewer, colorful ribbons, stolen by the waters from the cabinets we forgot to clean out, twirled and circled.

I rushed to the store. It was too late. It had been open all night, and they had sold out of pumps hours before I had arrived. At a nearby farm store, I successfully purchased one [stand] sump pump and thirty or so feet of soft blue rubber hosing and some clamps. I drove to another supply store on the other end of town, where I acquired their last submergible sump pump.

With the help of my neighbor and my wife, I got the two sump pumps running. Somehow I didn't get electrocuted, and the pumps stopped the water from rising.

Every ten minutes or so, the pumps would stop and I would rush downstairs and reset the circuit breaker. Eventually we started to hold our own against the rising waters. An hour later I got a second submergible, which I located at the sewer itself. Once it was installed, the water began to recede. By afternoon the waters in my basement had been defeated. Wearing my new green boots and manning my new, small-wheeled, tipsy, red shop vac, I stood triumphant over the receding waters. I had not been electrocuted, and around the sewer's hub colorful ribbons lay still.

The Gift of Sandbags

Joseph Amato

On a Saturday afternoon, under the shadow of the water tower on the edge of Justice Park, adjacent to the city maintenance sheds and building, less than a couple hundred yards from where the raging diversion channel rejoined the swollen Redwood River, a crowd with shovels gathered. They responded to phone calls and radio announcements that there was a need for volunteers to fill sandbags.

One group opened, tied, and stacked the new white plastic sand bags with attached cord strings, while another group filled the small bags.

The dump trucks did not keep pace with the workers. They spread out the sand they dropped, allowing more people to work along the line while making it easier to avoid being hit by the handle of a busy shovel.

Cars, vans, and pickup trucks appeared regularly. They picked up a load of sandbags and headed off to wherever they thought sandbags were needed. No priority was given.

A self-organized industry was at work. A community of work and goodwill had appeared. But, against the darkening sky looming in the west and the steadily rising waters, the efforts of the volunteers appeared frail and puny. At most, the sandbags they filled would defend very little.

Yet they shoveled on—parent and child, old and young, college president, mayor, and dentist worked shoulder-to-shoulder with the Schwan's assembly line worker and truck driver. They gave testimony to the fact that a lot of people like to work communally, and that the town is built on the bedrock of goodwill.

Marshall residents create a wall of sandbags

—Jerry Sowden,
Marshall Independent

In the Face of the Storm

Toni Beebout-Bladholm

The rains of May 6, 1993, were only a beginning for the residents of southwestern Minnesota and the Midwest. The wet and soggy conditions did not disappear as people had hoped, and the watery conditions continued for months. The amazing thing about floods is how they come in and shake up people's lives without notice or apology. In a rush-and-race world, there is no time for a crisis. Floods steal personal mementos, things of monetary value, and time.

Floods take things that can't be tallied or totaled, like a child's first grade paper, and memories. It is impossible to place a value on such precious things. Things that seem trivial become important when threatened with loss. Although most people deny that it could ever happen to them, reality is harsh and impossible to escape. Neighbors looked on as others hauled their possessions to curbs and street corners for pickup, thankful that it hadn't happened to them. Little did they realize that there was more to come and that their good fortune might not last.

The magnitude of events can be measured by the effects they have on people. The eyes of the people whose lives were turned upside down told the story. Emotions ran high, sometimes even higher than the water level. Communities can either come together or fall apart in the face of disaster. The communities of southwestern Minnesota pulled together under nearly impossible circumstances. A good example of this is the way people rallied together to protect their homes and communities by sandbagging. City officials organized available materials, private business owners donated supplies, and everyone pitched in on the labor. Young and old, rich and poor were brought together by the disaster. Sandbags salvaged homes, streets, parks, and various precious possessions. The cooperative efforts worked.

According to *The American Heritage Dictionary of The English Language*, the term sandbagging means: "A bag filled with sand and used as a ballast, in the formation of protective walls, or as a weapon." This definition doesn't seem to do sandbags justice. It would be more fitting if it said: "They were lifesavers, they protected homes and communities." The crisis clearly brought people together. The residents of southwestern Minnesota and the Midwest have reason to be proud of their efforts, whether it was through sandbagging or helping cook meals for those filling the bags; people stuck together and protected their communities.

> *"Become friends with your neighbors, because you never know when you are going to need their help. We all must learn to protect and help each other."*
>
> –James Zarzana

Vesta community members pull together to sandbag homes

–Redwood Gazette

Levees of Laughter

Janet Timmerman

After the sandbag battles had been fought, and the water had languidly receded of its own accord, in the midst of shock and exasperation, people began putting up levees of laughter. Laughter helps people endure hardships of all kinds. Laughter and keeping one's sense of humor about the situation may be what spurs a community's triumph over tragedy.

> "Even Noah got a break after forty days."
> –Pipestone County Star

Wherever weary flood-fighters gathered during and after the 1993 flood, a humorous story or joke would eventually cause smiles to break out. "Did you hear about the latest crop pest? Carp! How about the farmer who tried to pick corn in the rain? He got water in his ears!"

The floods played on people's sense of the ludicrous by radically changing their environment. Streets became streams, basements became pools, and fields became lakes. Perceptions were turned topsy-turvy. Children were the first to accept the changes with good humor, riding bikes in three feet of water or making the front porch into a diving platform. A makeshift raft could turn yesterday's fifth-grader into Huck Finn.

Adults clung to the sobriety of the situation longer, but eventually a glimmer of mirth appeared even in their dank surroundings. Some taped flood cartoons from the daily papers up on bulletin boards and refrigerators. Others sported T-shirts showing a farmer planting corn in scuba gear. Another put up a sign on the front yard claiming distant kinship to Noah. With a wry smile they turned to the work of rebuilding a life, a little less burdened by knowing that they laughed in the face of disaster.

–Reprinted with permission of the *Des Moines Register*

56

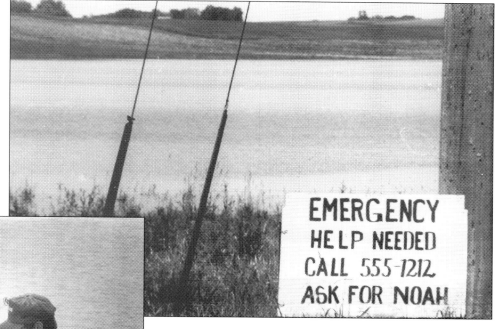

*Farmer posts a sign
near Tracy*
 –Tracy Headlight Herald

*A unique approach to planting
crops near Jackson*
 –Jackson County Pilot

57

Pumps, Pumps, and More Pumps

Joseph Amato

The floods of 1993 made me think about pumps more than I ever had before. The flood caused me to buy a new small pedestal pump and two new small submergible pumps (a type of pump that was brand new to me).

Pumps used in the city of Pipestone

–Pipestone County Star

On a street near the flooded Camelot Trailer Park, I saw a 55-horsepower (hp), 6-inch trash pump (a pump that can suck up rocks, stones, muck, and whatever) spewing 2,500 gallons per minute (gpm). I was told that the city had one other such pump, which broke down fighting the flood. In addition, the city had access to a standard portable 2½-inch electric pump of its own and another from the Department of Natural Resources. The Army Corps of Engineers even lent an 18-inch pump powered by a 75-hp motor, capable of pumping several million gallons a minute. At the time, however, it was stationed at Watson's Wastewater Treatment Plant, north of Montevideo.

After the flood, I began to see a new horizon of pumps in stores. Measured by horsepower, gallons per minute, and number of ports, they were made of metal and plastic (that wonderfully water-resistant material). These were pumps that stood up (pedestal pumps) or lay down in the water (submergible pumps); pumps powered by electricity, gasoline, and hydraulics; pumps that had their own motors and pumps that were attached to motors; and, in the farm supply stores, pumps that could be attached to a tractor. In my only technical book at home, *How Things Work*, I read about rotary pumps, gear pumps, centrifugal pumps, peristaltic pumps, and other kinds of pumps. A whole world of pumps and the valves, seals, and piping that service them bloomed in my mind.

I began to imagine everyone from Buffalo Ridge to New Orleans pumping with all sorts of pumps. They did this in concert with all the other devices we had for sucking up and sweeping away water and cleansing and sanitizing the places it had been. With this thought came the notion that we have changed the very nature of floods. Not only do we, with drainage channels and levees, gather and shape the floods that come from distant places, but we can also quickly overcome floods. We pump water out of our basements, off our streets, from our towns and farms, and into rivers and the great channels we have dug to sweep them away to the sea or to unfortunate places where either there are no levees, or the levees don't hold.

At least Marshall's 1993 floods—thanks to new, better, and more abundant pumps—proved to be a relatively quick affair. Unlike the 1957 flood, the town was not isolated for days, children were not sent off to camps and to relatives, cleaning up did not drag on for weeks, and the primary concern of the flood's effects was not contamination and typhoid. The Department of Health, accordingly, no longer plays the dominant role in flood clean-up it once did in times past.

All this made an odd sort of sense to me. From the beginning of agricultural civilization, to control the land has meant to attempt to control water. Industrial civilization, our civilization, has meant not only seeking further control of water (with dikes, dams, canals, and levees), but has also been about pumping machines, valves, and the movement of liquids. It stands to reason that we humans, the great transformers of nature, should try to control water. After all, at the beginning of time, we were willing to accept stolen fire.

> *"I hope it doesn't rain. Every time it does I say, 'Lord, don't let another sump pump burn up.'"*
> —Viola Rust

Large pumps used in the Marshall community
—Jerry Sowden, *Marshall Independent*

A Port In the Storm

Jennifer Mathiason

Pan Xiong, one of the people that came to the Red Cross shelter in Marshall, with her daughters

–Jean Stockwell,
Marshall Independent

Throughout its history, the American Red Cross has been a symbol of help. Early in May 1993, as it became apparent that the spring rains were not going to stop, the Red Cross once again came to help.

On May 8, East Side Elementary School became the designated Red Cross shelter for the continuing summer floods. Lyon County Red Cross Coordinator Linda Julien contacted Bill Swope, the school's principal, asking him to open the school for the shelter. He agreed, and, working closely with Frank Morse, the director of the Region VIII Welfare Office and the Lyon County Civil Defense director, Tammy VanOverbeke, the shelter's opening was announced over the radio.

Because of the enormous damage done during the first flood of the summer, the Minnesota State Red Cross was called in to help. Unfortunately, and as usual, as Julien noted, the state did not send in trained Red Cross shelter volunteers for over 50 hours. This left Julien and her 14-year-old son, the only trained volunteers, to run the shelter along with untrained community members. Once the state did take over on May 11, it did a fine job of providing the Marshall residents in need a dry place to sleep and plenty of food, soap, and clean water.

"It was the school reaching out to the community," said Swope. The Red Cross encouraged all of Marshall to reach out and to help itself and its people. McDonald's and the

Golden Corral restaurants provided the shelter with food. Moreover, Hy-Vee grocery store catered, at a lowered price, the meals during the first day the shelter was opened. The money for extras, such as coffee, bar soap, paper towels, diapers, and baby formula, came from the $12,000 provided by the National Red Cross. Cots were brought in from Garvin and Tracy. Fifty new pillows and blankets were donated by Marshall Wal-Mart. Homemade snacks, along with canned food and more blankets and pillows, came from Marshall residents. Approximately 20 to 30 community members worked as volunteers for the Red Cross during the summer months.

"At least we knew we could count on the Red Cross to be there for us," stated Camelot Trailer Park resident Shirleen Schwab. East Side Elementary School was opened as the site of the Red Cross emergency shelter three times during the summer of 1993. Besides being in operation for three long days during Mother's Day weekend, the shelter was re-opened June 16 and July 3. During the first flood, the Red Cross provided shelter, food, and clean water for over 100 people. Throughout the summer, over 90 percent of those helped were from Camelot Trailer Park. Marshall police officers drove trucks into the park, transporting many to the shelter the first night of the Mother's Day flood.

Members of the Lyon County chapter of the Red Cross are all trained volunteers and do not get paid for the services they provide. During the floods of 1993, the Red Cross was only given 10 to 15 trained people to be on hand to operate the shelter set-up at East Side. Julien stated that, "Those trained and able to operate a Red Cross shelter are few and far between." Yet, those few made a difference to many.

More Agencies Than You Can Shake A Stick At _____

Stacy Monge

How many agencies does it take to handle a flood? There are agencies such as the Army Corps of Engineers and the Soil Conservation Service that work to prevent floods. Then there are groups such as the American Red Cross, the Salvation Army, the Department of Commerce Division of Emergency Management, and numerous volunteer organizations that helped communities during the floods. Finally the Federal Emergency Management Agency, the Department of Housing and Urban Development, the Small Business Organization, along with a host of other federal, state, and local agencies helped monetarily and personally with the aftermath of what has been termed "The Great Flood of 1993." It takes more agencies than you can shake a stick at to handle a flood, as the following list, which is not exhaustive, illustrates.

National Agencies

Department of Agriculture:
    Agricultural Stabilization and
        Conservation Service
    Farmers Home Administration
    Federal Crop Insurance
        Corporation
    Food and Nutrition Service
    Rural Development Administration
    Soil Conservation Service
Department of Commerce:
    National Oceanic and Atmospheric
        Administration
    National Weather Service
Department of Defense,
    Army Corps of Engineers
Department of Education
Department of Energy
Department of Health and
    Human Services
Department of Housing and
    Urban Development
Department of Interior,
    U.S. Geological Survey

Department of Justice
Department of Labor
Department of State
Department of Transportation
Department of Treasury
Department of Veterans Affairs
American Red Cross
Salvation Army
Environmental Protection Agency
Federal Communications Commission
Federal Emergency Management Agency
General Services Administration
Interstate Commerce Commission
National Aeronautical and Space Administration
National Communications System
U.S. Economic Development Administration
Nuclear Regulatory Commission
Office of Personnel Management
Tennessee Valley Authority
U.S. Postal Service
Small Business Administration
Sierra Club
United Way

State Agencies

Department of Agriculture
Department of Administration:
    Division of Building Construction
    Bureau of Property Management
Department of Natural Resources:
    Division of Waters
    Division of Fish and Wildlife
    Division of Parks and Recreation
Department of Education
Higher Education Coordinating Board
University of Minnesota:
    Extension Services
    Minnesota State University System
Department of Public Safety,
    Division of Emergency Management
Department of Transportation
Board of Water and Soil Resources
Department of Jobs and Training
    Division of Jobs, Opportunities,
        and Insurance
Minnesota Historical Society
Pollution Control Agency
Department of Trade and
    Economic Development
Department of Health
Department of Human Services
Minnesota Geological Survey
Minnesota Housing Finance Agency
Office of the Attorney General
Office of the Governor
Minnesota State House of Representatives
Minnesota State Senate
Sustainable Farming Association of Minnesota
Land Stewardship Project
Association of Minnesota Counties
Minnesota Food Association
Minnesota Bankers Association
Minnesota Association of Townships

Local Agencies

Minnesota Legal Services
Private Industry Council
Regional Development Commissions
Western Human Development
Rural Partners in Prevention
Family Services
Project Turnabout
Project Noah
Women's Shelters
Lutheran Social Services
Community Nursing Services
Financial Institutions
Farm Advocates
Soil and Water Conservation Districts
County Enterprise Development Corporation
Alternative Career Planning–Mainstay
Area Churches and Ministerial Associations
Project Resource
Southwest Minnesota Housing Partnership
Housing and Redevelopment Authorities
County Commissioners
Township Boards
Western Community Action
Prairie V Community Action
Lac Qui Parle-Yellow Bank Watershed District
Yellow Medicine River Watershed District
Kanaranzi-Little Rock Watershed District
Middle Des Moines Watershed District
Okabena-Ocheda Watershed District
Cottonwood River Association
Redwood River Area Association
Southwest Minnesota Opportunity Council
Southwest Regional Development Commission
Region VIII North Welfare
Area II Minnesota River Basin Projects, Inc.
Redwood-Cottonwood Rivers Control Area
Weiner Memorial Medical Center
Insurance Agencies
County Environmental Offices
County Emergency Management
City Offices and Utilities
Local Media
Amateur Radio Clubs
Law Enforcement and Fire Departments
Public Schools

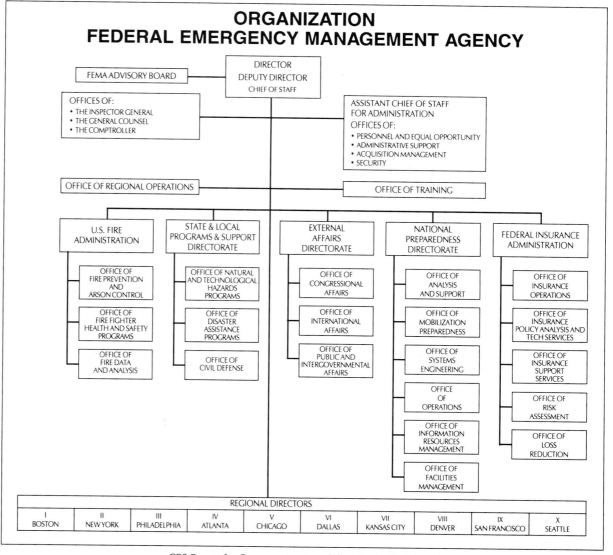

–CRS Report for Congress, FEMA and the Disaster Relief Fund

An Agency's Work Is Never Done

Stacy Monge

Before the floods of 1993, there were agencies. During the flood of 1993, there were more agencies. After the flood of 1993, there were even more agencies. Floods and other disasters have become entangled within a web of bureaucracy. Hundreds of agencies work to control, prevent, and clean up flood damage.

Prior to the 1993 flood, the Army Corps of Engineers, the Soil Conservation Service, the Department of Natural Resources, Watershed Districts, and Area II Minnesota River Basin Projects, Inc., worked to prevent future floods. They did this by building diversion channels and dams, restoring wetlands, and encouraging farming practices that are conducive to retaining floodwaters. Corps of Engineers and Soil Conservation Service projects helped to avert an estimated $118 million in potential damages in Minnesota during the 1993 floods. Local agencies and groups worked to help communities and farmers; state and federal agencies provided technical and monetary assistance, and protected the environmental and legal interests of the state and nation.

As the floodwaters continued to rise in southwestern Minnesota, so did the number of agencies and groups involved. Volunteer organizations such as the Red Cross, the Salvation Army, and local churches set up shelters immediately to help those forced from their homes by the water. The Federal Emergency Management Agency (FEMA), the Minnesota Department of Public Safety—Division of Emergency Management, and local emergency-management teams organized relief efforts. Disaster application centers opened to help individuals apply for state and federal assistance, and disaster field offices were set up to house the multitude of agencies offering assistance. The State Emergency Operations Center installed a telephone disaster hotline to direct people to the proper agency, which could provide the help they needed, ranging from home repair to psychological counseling. The flooding caused many agencies to form temporary groups to assess the needs of the public, as well as to fill in gaps in the system. Local agencies were the backbone of the relief efforts. Located in the affected communities, they were the first to respond and help out when neighbors joined together to help pile sandbags and salvage whatever they could from water-filled homes, churches, schools, farms, and businesses.

In the aftermath of any disaster, the big question is, "Who is going to pay for this?" Agencies which were most visible were FEMA and the many branches of the U.S. Department of Agriculture—the Farmers Home Administration, the Agricultural Stabilization and Conservation Service, and the Soil Conservation Service. The federal government contributed $573.5 million to help Minnesota recover. Money was available through the state and federal levels of the Department of Education to help reopen schools, as well as to help college students whose families lost income due to the floods. The Department of Jobs and Services helped farmers by providing unemployment payments and by helping them find alternate work. Local agencies, such as the Southwest Regional Development Commission, coordinated federal and state relief efforts. They made the mountain of paperwork easier by helping fill out forms and guiding families and communities through the maze of official red tape.

The flood was a learning experience for agencies at all levels. The Division of Emergency Management, the Department of Commerce, and a federal interagency task force each published recommendations on how to improve emergency management for future disasters. The Army Corps of Engineers and their state and local counterparts worked to improve flood control measures. If agencies had nothing else in common, at least they had this—"every group at the federal, state, and local level wished to put an end to the extensive suffering and damage caused by disasters like the flood of 1993."

Don and Betty Verkinderen, who farm near Marshall, visit the disaster application center

—Jerry Sowden, *Marshall Independent*

How to Spell Relief: M-O-N-E-Y

Rebecca Schlorf

Farmers look to the government in bad times, and the floods of 1993 were no exception. Farmers felt the government should help them, and the government, in the habit of aiding farmers since the 1930s, concurred. Most farmers

A Redwood area farmer participates in the 0/92 farm program

–Redwood Gazette

did not have crop insurance to cover losses from the 1993 flooding. The entire crop insurance plan is not very well formulated. Many farmers in 1993 counted on government aid, whether they had federal flood insurance or not. On the basis of a small representative sample of farmers, the

Southwestern Minnesota Farm Management Association estimated that a third of farmers lost ground financially due to crop losses, and half could not pay their living expenses from their 1993 farm income.

The United States Department of Agriculture (USDA) offered Prevented Planting Credit, Failed Acreage Credit and 0/92 to farmers that were in the farm program. These programs were of little help to farmers. More money had to be made available as the damage progressed. Farmers Home Administration (FmHA) was given the mandate to help farmers in need with low-interest loans. In July, the USDA extended the 0/92 deadline to September 17 to allow more farmers to sign up.

Farmers who signed up by the extended 0/92 deadline of September 17 had to plow under their crops in order to obtain 72 cents per bushel on three-fourths the corn base for 92 percent of the land. Farmers struggled with the decision, some waiting until the final hours before the deadline to decide whether or not to destroy their crops. All together, about 923,000 acres of Minnesota corn, wheat, barley, and oats were plowed under in the hope of breaking even.

Conservation easements (Reinvest In Minnesota and Permanent Wetland Preserves Program) through the Minnesota Board of Water and Soil Resources (BWSR) were pushed on flooded cropland. In normal years, payments might not be received for up to nine months after making application. In 1993, more money was made available through disaster relief and ad hoc legislation in Congress to allow payments to be received shortly after sign-up so more land might be enrolled.

Livestock owners were not as directly affected by the floods as crop farmers. They could take advantage of the conservation easements and enroll land, or they had the Livestock Feed Program and Crop Disaster available to help them. A loss of greater than 40 percent of the crop in the county made the Livestock Feed Program available without an act of Congress.

The ad hoc disaster legislation for the floods of 1993 was greater than the all-time high of $4 billion, which was allocated for the drought of 1988. (The exact dollar amount has not yet been calculated.) This edged Congress one more step closer to restructuring the federal crop insurance program and eliminating ad hoc legislation. The Federal Crop Insurance Reform Act of 1994 combined the USDA crop insurance and the disaster assistance programs and will be administered by the Agricultural Stabilization and Conservation Service as one program. All producers are required to obtain catastrophic crop insurance coverage in order to benefit from USDA programs. Producers pay a $50 processing fee per crop. This is a more reliable and predictable system of coverage by the federal government for disaster situations.

With the good crop and weather of 1994, many farmers put the flooded year of 1993 behind them. The difference

"Rain makes grain."
–Alison Cummings

THE FLOOD OF 1993   THE FLOOD OF 1994

between the crop years is well represented in the cartoon showing a grain storage bin overflowing in 1994, compared to the other half of the cartoon representing the flood of 1993 with an overflow of water.

–Reprinted with permission of the *Des Moines Register*

The Floods Turned Everyone Into a Psychologist or a Patient

Social Services in the Floods of 1993

Units of Service Provided by Category (Lincoln, Lyon, Murray, Redwood, Yellow Medicine)

Services Provided	Assessment & Screening	Information & Referral	Individual Counseling	Group Counseling	Advocacy & Coordination	24-Hour Crisis Line	Other
Total # Units of Service	35	477	9	13	274	0	6

Number Served by Presenting Problem Type

Problem Type	Stress Anxiety Depression	Children Having Difficulty	Anger	Disaster Fears	Adults Acting Out	Need for Information	Family Disruption	Alcohol & Drug Abuse	Other
# Served	15	11	1	0	0	760	0	0	3

Group Services, Number of Groups Served and Number of People Served in Groups

Type of Group	Neighborhood	School Students	School Staff	Human Service Staff	Disaster Workers	Other
# of Groups Served	11	1	3	8	0	17
# Served in Groups	52	13	62	151	0	221

Number of Clients Served by Gender

Type of Client	# of Clients Served
Male	359
Female	431

–From the Department of Human Services Minnesota Flood Support Services Program and Marshall's "Project Resource"

We are now in an age where good health includes mental well-being. Thus, it is no surprise that as the rains fell and the rivers escaped their banks, saturating much of the Midwest, agencies tried to help people save their minds as well as their property. Even before President Clinton declared any portion of Minnesota to be in a state of emergency, the Minnesota Flood Support Services Program (MFSSP) set up an unofficial Crisis Counseling Program (CCP) to assist individuals, families, and communities in using the resources available to help them adjust to and recover from the impact of the floods. On May 6, 1993, the CCP sent out information to regional mental health centers in places already hit by flooding. This included instructions for trained psychologists and mental health workers. The information also explained to community members how to spot neighbors in trouble and how to get them help. The floods of 1993 had bankers, cafe owners, waiters, waitresses, Minnesota Extension Service staff, ministers, school teachers, and lawyers acting as mental health workers.

In 1993, with the total dollar amount of damage to crops equaling $1.5 billion, the Midwestern farmers were the most financially devastated during the floods of 1993. Consequently, they were also the ones most likely to need more than just financial help. The MFSSP wanted to create an organization that would reach out to farm families. In July, through the MFSSP, the CCP received a grant of $420,000 to set up a "Farm Advocates Group." In this project, outreach workers were educated on ways to spot and help individuals and families that seemed to need help. These workers included farmers, agricultural seed dealers, farm equipment distributors, and others who would be most likely to attend functions where farmers gathered. The Farm Advocates Group also offered support to the agriculture lenders.

In July the Mental Health Division of the Department of Human Services also provided a grant worth $50,000, $10,000 of which went to each of the five mental health centers in the areas of Minnesota most affected by the floods. The Western Human Development Center in Marshall, which serves Yellow Medicine, Lincoln, Lyon, Redwood, and Murray counties, used this money to set up "Project Re-source." Under the direction of Shirley Peotter, the project hired outreach workers to locate those in need of assistance, to provide education, to distribute literature, and to operate a hotline. Overall, "Project Resource" served 791 people.

The CCP, working under the Minnesota Flood Support Services Program, could not help everyone. Minnesota counted a total of four suicides, the majority being farmers who, possibly because of the added stress, could not handle the additional problems caused by the floods. This was the highest number of all the midwestern states.

Overall, the amount of money spent by the CCP in Minnesota from May 1993 to February 14, 1994, totaled $823,817.22. The question remains however, whether the counseling offered was effective in the short or long term. This would, of course, be difficult to assess.

Live Eye

Toni Beebout-Bladholm and Jennifer Mathiason

Unlike most disasters, floods lend themselves to prediction and precision. Tornadoes skip and veer, and hurricanes and blizzards seem to move at whim. But a flood has only one way to go, and it usually follows a schedule. Because of this, and because of the sheer number of people affected, floods lend themselves to on-going media coverage. In turn,

WCCO Live Eye in the Sky visits Tracy during the flood of 1993
–Tracy Headlight Herald

the way the nation viewed these events depended on how the print and electronic media covered them.

The media's significance in the flood of 1993 was increased by the massive amount of video footage available.

Within hours of a disaster, crews were on the site. This immediate response was due to advances in technology.

In the past, the media was forced to rely on the printed word. Pictures were often of poor quality and were too expensive to print. With improved technology, however, the media has gained power. The advances made in video cameras, and the creation of mobile satellites and computer-based print technology has allowed the media to visually record and manipulate the perceptions of more and more events more quickly. The media's coverage of the 1993 flooding in the Midwest proves to be a good example of its increasing power over the way we perceive and interpret the events that take place in our world. Technological advances made the retrieval and presentation of information much easier and much more dramatic in 1993 than in past floods. At the same time, the massive amounts of information meant that, more than ever, media coverage was about the selection of information.

The use of photos and videotape was a major factor in the way the 1993 flood was viewed. In the past, the media relied on words to convey information about disasters. As news became more and more visual, the public response and empathy to disaster increased. The media's role in the 1993 flood affected the way the rest of the nation saw the disaster. For example, the community of Marshall received a lot of attention during the summer of 1993. Prior to these events, the city had never received such massive national attention. Media attention complicated the situation during the floods of 1993. The victims of the 1993 flood were bombarded by constant requests for interviews. Gail Peavey, a resident of Marshall, said that the press was a constant concern of hers. The media frequently bothered her with trivial questions like, "How are you doing?" The answer was obvious to her since her home was being inundated by water. To Peavey, the media seemed insensitive. Yet at the same time, it dramatized events.

The media also skewed the way in which area communities were presented. For example, in Marshall, the media presented Camelot Trailer Park as an area representative of the condition of the whole town. By shooting this area, the one neighborhood that Marshall residents often neglected, shows how the media can determine how the rest of the nation perceived flooded midwestern towns, versus how the communities saw themselves.

Because news is a business that sells a product, the news made the floods flashy, dramatic, and sensational. For the media, evoking emotion helps sell the product, and so the flood of 1993 was displayed by the media in the most emotional way possible. The real pain felt by flood victims was exploited for profit. Victimization was a constant theme in television, radio, newspapers, magazines, and talk shows. Through these events, the nation saw children lose their homes and families fighting to save their communities, cities, and keepsakes.

This dramatization, however, had some useful effects. It brought donations of money, supplies, and other forms of support into areas of need. The media demonstrated a need and people responded.

One of the biggest differences between the flood of 1993 and those of the past was how the media shaped the perception of the public. The media gave people a single, common memory that will represent the flood of 1993 for years to come. A flood may just be a flood, but in conjunction with the media, a flood can be a form of entertainment.

News crew assesses flood damage in Pipestone by rowboat
–Pipestone County Star

Floods Are Not All Bad

Joseph Amato

During and after the 1993 floods, Marshall's True Value Home Center sold 1,068 sump pumps, 2,073 discharge kits, and 440 check valves. Their usual sales for these items in the same three-month period were from 50 to 75 each. True Value sold 300 shop vacs, instead of the usual 10 to 15, and 65 squeegees, rather than the typical 3 to 5. True Value also sold staggering amounts of clamps, piping, and valves to desperate people whose flooded and sewage-filled basements turned them into amateur plumbers. Carpet sales exceeded all norms.

One woman bought brand-new carpeting for her downstairs, only to get it installed in time for the second flood. She did, however, wait until October to buy new tile for her basement.

For the exterior of homes, True Value sold 24,000 linear feet of rain gutter and 4,000 feet of downspout, ten times the average amount sold. Shingle sales increased four-fold to 2,200,000 square feet, enough to fill 100 semis.

Other hardware stores had similar sales records. Pumps, hoses, clamps, detergents, soap, boots, buckets—anything that would remove water, clean up its damage, or replace what the flood and hail ruined, sold. Insurance adjusters, plumbers, carpenters, painters, roofers—both from the region and drawn from outside the region—found ample work in Marshall, while hardware, furniture, appliance, carpet, and paint salespeople prospered—not from price gouging (at least none was reported)—but from the sheer struggle to throw the water out and to return the homes of a city and a countryside to normal.

Certain losses associated with the flood—like the water-logged family album and the confidence in the very security of one's home—were beyond compensation. Yet, as in most disasters, money was made. Not every settlement was to the disadvantage of the owner. Marshall experienced a small boom in building and business, thanks to the terrible floods of 1993.

Marshall business advertisements

–Marshall Independent

Ecologists Upstream, Engineers Downstream

Joseph Amato

In the rural Midwest, where getting rid of water has been the essence of agriculture for over a century, where the miles of drainage ditches equal the miles of roads in some counties, and where by law every person has the right to let water follow its natural path across the land, neighbors fear one another's water. Loss of land means loss of livelihood. Unlike the West—where drought prevails and irrigation commands—the strongest accusation among midwestern farmers, which has more than once been delivered with the display of a shotgun, is: "You're flooding me out."

The draining of a small slough, the installation of tiling, the digging or cleaning of a ditch, or setting the elevation of a road or dam, can become a decade-long battle. County, city, and township officials, as well as the Department of Natural Resources, the Army Corps of Engineers, and even the Pollution Control Agency—contibute to making the history of drainage the story of long grudges and deep acrimonies. At local coffee shops where farmers gather, one only has to name a county or judicial ditch number to see sparks fly.

Floods like those in 1993 exacerbate standing divisions over water. Farmers upstream hurry their waters downstream. Farmers immediately to the south of Marshall, in the Cottonwood Plain (which received part of the flood-swollen Redwood River), are terrified that besieged Marshall (defending itself at its western border) will break through Highway 23 and shunt the Redwood River water south onto them. In turn, farmers to the north and east receive the rejoined waters of the Redwood River and the city's diversion channel, which comes from the growing city in ever greater quantities and more quickly.

Farmers and city dwellers alike look upstream for their solution, even though all three flood events in 1993 were different. Their hopes lay in buying and renting farmlands that were once lakebeds, they project creating and extending wetlands (as is argued in the case of RW-22), or they hope to build roads that cross ravines and gullies to serve as temporary dams to slow and accumulate waters. In turn, people downstream along the Minnesota and Mississippi, while keeping their own levees, see an increasing need for the reinstitution of wetlands and natural flooding upstream.

From Buffalo Ridge to New Orleans, it seems that the general principle is: "You keep as much water as you can, while I will get rid of as much as quickly as I can." Or, "Nature for you and a levee for me." Or, "Let us all be ecologists upstream and engineers downstream."

*Goose nesting mound in a
water retention area*

–Office of Lyon County Engineer

*Road retention
overflow weir*

–Office of Lyon County Engineer

What About This RW-22

Jim Muchlinski

After the 1993 flood, it's hard to be non-committal about flood control. A disastrous spring and summer was more than enough to create a demand for answers.

A regional joint-powers group known as Area II believes it may have an answer, with a proposal for a massive retention dam at the southern edge of Lyon County between Florence and Balaton. Many people living north of the dam-site, known as RW-22, endorsed the idea as a centerpiece to regional flood control. Others remained unconvinced, particularly a group of landowners living in the vicinity.

The area around RW-22 is part of a glacial moraine, where Ice Age glacial advance ended and left a line of hills. The Redwood River later carved a path through the hills on its way toward Marshall. Among those hills a large pooling area could be created once a dam is installed.

"It won't take much of a dam to build," said Minnesota Board of Water and Soil Resources Chief Engineer Al Kean in a January 1994 article published in the *Marshall Independent.* "Mother Nature has already done much of the work."

At its maximum capacity, which would be reached in storms similar to the May and June floods of 1993, the pooling area behind RW-22 would cover 1,400 acres. It would extend over a portion of Lyon County Road 12, a group of township roads, and property owned by more than 20 landowners.

Area II, after sponsoring more than $4.5 million in water projects over a nine-county area since 1980, was publicly confident that the $2.2 million RW-22 project would succeed in getting the needed state funding.

"We're not really too concerned," Area II administrator Kerry Netzke told the *Independent* in January 1994. "There is a good feeling about this project. With legislators believing in the project it will get funded." State legislators from the Marshall area and Lyon County's Board of Commissioners played leading roles in supporting the project during 1993 and 1994.

"We have a definite need for it, and we'll need to do whatever we can to make sure it moves forward," said State Senator Arlene Lesewski (Independent Republican-Marshall) during a conservation road tour in southern Lyon County in August 1993.

Opposition to the project remained equally intense. Balaton area landowner Wally Wichmann, who favors RW-22 and would allow the dam to be built on his property, acknowledged that the project drove neighbors apart, at one point admitting that "those guys won't even talk to me."

Landowners against RW-22 objected to the idea of flooding roads, farm buildings, cropland, and pastures, and only being compensated with an easement payment. "If that county road gets flooded, a lot more than 23 landowners will be hollering," said Balaton area resident Paul Erickson. "In my opinion, this is a powder keg ready to explode."

Those not wanting to agree to a flood easement could face the prospect of having land condemned through eminent domain. In discussing the issue of compensation in a

February 1994 article, Netzke noted that easement offers would have definite limits. "What do they feel will be fair? More," she said. "It is natural on their own property to value it more than the outside world, it is human nature."

As 1994 drew to a close, the RW-22 debate appeared ready to enter a new phase. Agency reviews of the proposal were nearing completion. A public opportunity to submit formal comments, long awaited by many residents, would help to shape the future of RW-22, as well as regional flood control. Controversy over water remains long after floodwaters have receded.

Redwood River Watershed

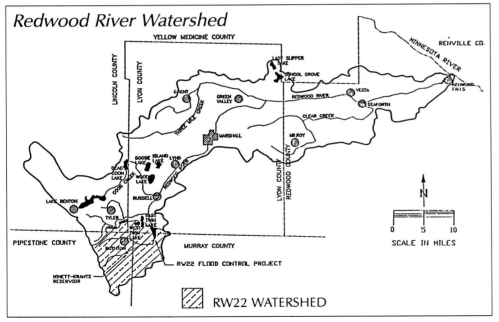

–Based on Floodwater Retarding Structures and Levee Instigations Map, Redwood River, Upper Minnesota River Subbasins Study (Public Law 87-639) Jan. 1980

Public Forum

Thinks RW-22 a bad idea

"We won" was the (tone of the) editorial in the Marshall paper regarding RW-22. Eight hundred thousand dollars for the project, Ruthton protesters get beat, Marshall farmers and city folk are saved.

Fact 1: You haven't won anything because the Ruthton community and landowners, 22 out of 23, own the land. If the 22 landowners stay united and don't sign anything the RW-22 or Marshall dry dam is dead. They have the power, not you!

Fact 2: DNR is not dragging its feet, Mr. Feda. The DNR knows this useless project will destroy a wetland and that's why it is against it.

Fact 3: Army Corps is not for RW-22 as Sen. Lesewski said. Army Corps is for flood control, subject to social and environmental concerns. I wrote and asked about the Lesewski quote.

Fact 4: This is the best news for Marshall and Lyon County. The $800,000 can be used for alternate sites and county projects like Balaton's newly-created flood control, wetland area. Yes, you are reading this correctly. The $800,000 can be used for any project Area II thinks will benefit all of the people in southwestern Minnesota. Source of this information is Rep. Andy Steensma.

Rep. Steensma has worked very hard for not just his people in the Ruthton area but has looked at the concerns of the Marshall people as well as getting this money. As I talked with him he mentioned that if the projects are worthwhile, he was almost certain he could get more funding next time a funding bill comes up.

Lyon County commissioners, it is time to roll up your sleeves and give Area II some direction. Here is an idea. Call the township supervisors to a county meeting and ask them to find land to purchase and bridges that need fixing. This way you are doing two jobs at once— land for flood control and bridge repair. The people will see their tax dollars at work for good projects which will create wetlands as well.

The Ruthton area has a reservoir and a wetland base which doesn't cause a problem. The commissioners saw that with the slides shown at the last meeting of concerned landowners. Where are the plans for a Marshall reservoir or dikes? You are upstream from somebody.

Lynn Wichmann, Balaton

–May 26, 1994, *Marshall Independent*

Letting Go

Julie Porter and Rebecca Schlorf

Flooding is a natural process in ecosystems that enables the survival of species and the survival of the natural environment. Flooding provides many advantages for the environment. It allows for connections between streams, rivers, backwaters, wetlands, and lakes, which, in turn, enables ecological diversity. Migrating waterfowl and plant species depend on seasonal flooding. Waterfowl often use flooded fields or cropland for food and rest. Aquatic plant species depend on annual flooding and drawdowns, which expose mudflats where seeds can germinate and new plants can take hold. Fish sometimes depend on flooding in order to migrate upstream to spawning areas. Seasonally flooded wetlands or backwaters also filter and help purify water and hold excess water.

Humans are naturally cushioned from the overflow of a body of water by a floodplain. Floodplains have often been built on because of their scenic views or farmed due to excellent soil nutrients. When left in their natural states, floodplains have many benefits, but these benefits often go unrecognized. Because they provide space for temporary storage of excess water, floodplains are vital to the environment. They are also a source of erosion control. Floodplains provide a habitat and a variety of vegetation for many different species of fish and animals. Vegetation reduces erosion by binding soil with plant root systems. Also, the friction between plants and water on a floodplain reduces waves and the velocity of channels. Unaltered floodplains and banks can reduce flood velocities, flood peaks, and wind and wave impacts, thus reducing potential damages from flooding.

River systems follow routes that coincide with nature, which may or may not coincide with human economic or social interests. The common view throughout the history of the United States has been that human beings should use and alter the natural environment to meet their needs. Throughout history people have settled on the banks of rivers and streams, taking advantage of the wildlife, land, water supply, and other bounties that water sources provide. Unfortunately, development on floodplains sometimes causes damage to nature and people alike.

> *"The erosive power of running water is enormous and has been shaping the Earth's features ever since the planet's first rains. In its natural development a mature river is both destroyer and builder."*
>
> –Herbert Wendt

To protect ourselves and our property, we have tried to control runoff by building dams, reservoirs, levees, flood walls, and stream channels. These projects can do great damage to the environment by altering natural cycles. Millions of acres of wetlands have already been drained or filled, causing a significant loss of natural flood-storage areas, groundwater filtration, and wildlife species.

In the late nineteenth century, the United States Army Corps of Engineers built thousands of dams to make the Mississippi River channel narrower and deeper in order to carry barges. Earlier the Mississippi meandered freely across its vast floodplain. The building of locks and dams to improve commercial navigation may have improved transportation along waterways, but it stopped the natural processes that keep the river alive. Many species that once had been abundant in the Mississippi's waters have since disappeared, like the skipjack herring. During the flood of 1993, when dam gates were opened to relieve floodwaters, some skipjack herring were found once again in Minnesota waters. Although they quickly disappeared, this shows that if their movements were not restrained, they could once again be abundant.

We need to understand thoroughly potamology, the science of rivers, streams, and floodplains, if we are going to manipulate the environment to fit our needs and desires. It requires a view of the river ecosystem defined not by state or district lines, but by the essence of a river, the watershed. We need to establish a holistic view of rivers and the environment, including everything from hydrology and ecology to agronomy and socioeconomical factors, in order to comprehend and cooperate with nature. Politicians, citizens, and scientists need to know the situation at hand and deal with solutions and consequences together. People need to try to co-exist with the natural environment.

Humanity expects to harness the waters of nature with dams, levees, and flood walls and to remain out of the reach of natural forces and make life more stable, predictable, and liveable. When we inhabit the floodplain and destroy the wetlands and the amount of surface area for drainage, we cannot escape the fact that there will be consequences. The more we infringe on the course of rivers, the more they will infringe on us.

*Inundated signpost
near Marshall*

–Jerry Sowden,
Marshall Independent

The Mirror of Responsibility

Stacy Monge

Who or what was responsible for the flood of 1993? "Nature" poured excessive spring and summer rains upon land already saturated by massive amounts of snow dumped during the winter. It was nature's fault. Earlier generations drained many of the lakes and natural wetlands that once served to store excess water during spring thaws and summer rains. It was their fault. The Army Corps of Engineers built faulty dams, levees, and diversion channels. It is to blame. Government at all levels, with all of its "protective agencies," failed to fund the right projects that would have helped alleviate the damages done during the massive flooding. Farmers have tiled their fields extensively and dug ditches to carry their excess water to the rivers. They are far from innocent.

It is easy to see how we all make others responsible for catastrophes like the floods of 1993. If "they" had not done this, or if "they" had done that, things may not have gotten so out of hand. We rarely stop to think of what we may have done to contribute to the situation. Everyone who was flooded during the spring and summer of 1993 is in some way responsible for their own flooding. We choose to live on a floodplain. Rivers are not going to stop overflowing their banks and rains are not going to refrain from replenishing the water supply just because humans have moved into the neighborhood.

Beavers build dams, alter the environment for their benefit, and move on once the dam is washed out. The alterations serve the beavers as well as many other aquatic plants and animals that are given the chance to replenish their species. Human dams and levees have been installed mainly to service the immediate needs of humans. Little thought has been given to the environment, although that is starting to change. People have a hard time moving on after they have been flooded out. We put ourselves in the position to be flooded, just as the beaver does, yet we do not share the beaver's versatility. We take the water's challenge and attempt to tame it rather than accept the course of nature and adapt.

In his book *The Romance of Water*, Herbert Wendt wrote, "Throughout the prehistoric period and then through History itself, man has been familiar with the element and elemental force of water. He has sought it out, striven with it; worshipped it and, with the aid of technology, tamed it. This struggle against water and with water, bulking so large in the story of all peoples and all lands, has reached its climax in the building of audacious works." Instead of learning to adapt and move on, this battle with water has led us to build bigger dams and deeper ditches. This inability to adapt, along with numerous failed attempts to control water, has helped us to hand off responsibility. If we cannot do it, someone else should, but when someone else tries to take responsibility, they never seem to do the job to everyone's satisfaction. Therefore, in order to succeed in the struggle and reach an acceptable end, we must all take an active role and accept some of the responsibility.

Our attempts to control where water goes and how fast it gets there raise many ethical questions. Are we attempting to benefit the many, the few, or the one? Who are humans to dictate the course of nature? By controlling water, are we attempting to enhance or destroy the environment? Are we taking into consideration the full scope of our actions? When diverting or channeling water, do we stop to consider what we are passing on to those downstream? Are our actions today going to be of any benefit to future generations, or are they going to make the situation worse? The ethics of water control can be found at the heart of these controversies. The individual asks, "How will this action benefit me?" If only a few benefit from an action, the majority asks, "Why should we help pay for it?" When the

Field erosion near Marshall

  –Lois Winter

majority benefit at the expense of a few, in the form of added property flooding, the hurt few ask, "What about us?" It usually comes back to the individual. It is hard for us to see the big picture or the cumulative benefits of flood control when our own homes, businesses, and fields are being flooded.

Chief Seattle said, "This we know . . . the earth does not belong to Man; all things are connected like the blood which unites one family. Man did not weave the web of Life; he is merely a strand in it. Whatever he does to the web he does to himself." We must be able to survive as a part of nature. Living on floodplains and taking advantage of everything they have to offer has helped us survive. Controlling water is also a survival mechanism necessary to ensure agricultural productivity and the food supply. Continuously flooded fields yield low crops. Low yields raise the market value of corn and beans, and everyone pays higher prices to eat. Controlling water is unavoidable. It is the manner in which we control it and the considerations that we allow the environment that make our attempts at control ethical or unethical. Whatever we do to our surroundings, or whatever we do to others, we also do to ourselves. If we continue to straighten rivers, drain wetlands, and adversely alter nature, what kind of world are we building for the future? Will future generations know rivers that gracefully meander across the countryside? Or are they going to know rivers lined with concrete that stay neatly within their defined boundaries, only to erupt into a rage when the rains force them to overflow their banks? We value the beauty of nature. It is reflected in the prices of homes along lakes or rivers. Like the beaver, we must learn to live with water, instead of against it. Part of taking responsibility for our own flooding is learning to accept losses in favor of a greater good for the environment and for our neighbors. We cannot just pump water off our property and let those downstream deal with it, or rely on others to deal with the situation for us.

An Education for a City

Joseph Amato

The 1993 floods educated Marshall to new needs. First, the city needed to minimize the volume of water it would receive during a flood. The city sought to entrap and hold water upstream. It focused particular attention on the RW-22 project, a controversial project on the Redwood River which, if carried out, would transform a ravine and large wetland into a storage pond during future flood events.

Second, responding to the way in which the floodwaters of the river, rejoined by the waters of the diversion channel, reinfiltrated the northeastern edge of the city, the city has

Water breaching a sandbag dike near County Road 7

—Jerry Sowden,
Marshall Independent

81

intensified its political efforts to encourage the Army Corps of Engineers to complete the diversion channel, so that it will cover the entire northern circumference of the city.

Third, admitting how the growth of the city increases the amount of water it discharges into the countryside, the city has entered into a discussion with the farmers to the north and east of town to regulate its overflow waters more carefully.

Fourth, the city has retained an environmental engineering firm that has proposed what, no doubt, will prove a controversial policy to form a utility that will regulate and tax runoff waters. The policy would tax properties on the basis of their runoff, which is determined by the property's size and surface.

Fifth, and most significantly, the city has responded to the greatest victims of the flood—those whose basements were flooded with sewage three times in 1993 and, in many instances, again in 1994. To mitigate the pain of its citizens, the city has built a new sewage line and lift station serving the southern end of town. A thorough investigation of the present sewage system for structural deficiencies, blockage, faulty piping, leaking manhole covers, and other infiltration from foundations, sump pumps, and surface runoffs was begun. Additionally, Marshall considered unexpected inflow contributors (like Village Park I and II), insufficient hydraulic capacities, storm sewer upgrade in the case of County Ditch 62, and a surface water management plan.

Nevertheless, even when and if all these recommendations are carried out, 30-year storms will simply exceed the utility's design. This means that in great storms, like those of 1993 and 1957, the city will be covered with ponds, and basements will be filled with sewage.

In its main outlines, the flood's education is clear for the city and its residents: there is a price to be paid for building on the floodplain. Even when the town escapes floods from without, thanks to levees and diversion channels, it will not avert floods from within. The burdens of these floods from within, born of surface runoff and excess sewage, will not be equally shared. Some, simply by location, will receive the water and sewage of others. Some, to avoid the sewage of others, will use valves (whose installation is already encouraged by the city) to wall themselves from the sewage of others.

At this point the education of the flood is no longer clear. Instead, it has become morally ambivalent. It teaches that the price of community involves unequal sharing of goods and evils, waters and wastes.

Plain Sense

"The time has come to face the fact that this nation can no longer afford the high costs of natural disasters. We can no longer afford the economic costs to the American taxpayer, nor can we afford the social costs to our communities and individuals," Federal Emergency Management Agency Director James L. Witt testified to Congress. The luxury of living on floodplains has cost American taxpayers $573.5 million just for the state of Minnesota. The nationwide total is over $4.2 trillion. The amount continues to rise as more cities, counties, agencies, and other groups file for assistance with hazard mitigation projects and relief programs. The money received so far by southwestern Minnesota is in excess of $10 million.

Living on a floodplain has many benefits. Its soil is rich in nutrients, making it a profitable area for farming. The rivers of the floodplain provide steady sources of recreation and, in some cases, power. The floodplain creates aesthetically pleasing areas on which to build homes. The lakes are also recreational sources and add to the price of a house. Floodplains regenerate the groundwater supply. But the benefits come at a price, economically, socially, and ecologically.

Efficient management is needed if the cost of living on a floodplain is to decline. The federal government, through the National Flood Insurance Program, has worked to map out flood-prone areas for insurance reasons, as well as for floodplain management. The maps are used as guidelines for pricing flood insurance and for regulating the development of floodplains. It is up to the state and local governments to create and enforce regulations regarding the de-

velopment of floodplains. In Minnesota, the Department of Natural Resources has regulatory power over floodplain development. Despite the regulations, areas continue to over-develop the floodplain. In some cases, government-subsidized housing or private trailer courts are placed within the 100-year floodzone because the land is cheap—sometimes costing only one dollar per acre. Many of the people living in these areas fail to purchase flood insurance because they are unaware that they are required to purchase it when developing near the river. People are also reluctant to spend any more on added insurance.

The Federal Emergency Management Agency noted, "It is explicitly recognized that conditions at one floodplain location are generally interdependent upon locations and events elsewhere in the river . . . and in the total community of which the floodplain is a part." The flood of 1993 demonstrated the lack of efficient floodplain management in upstream areas. Development has caused more runoff to enter the river systems as the result of extensive ditching, tiling, draining of wetlands, paving roads and parking lots, and pumping water off of property that once served to hold back waters. We are in the habit of passing our unwanted water on to our neighbors. This does little to cement social relationships, and conflicts arise between upstream and downstream communities. When managing floodplains it is essential to take into account that what is done upstream can greatly help or harm those living downstream.

> *"Probability is a planner's tool and does not govern the weather."*
>
> –L. Sowles

Overdeveloping floodplains also has detrimental ecological costs. Thousands of acres of wetlands are lost, leading to greater flood problems. The loss of wetlands greatly affects the groundwater supply, leaving us with less fresh water.

Flooded home near Morton

–Redwood Gazette

Wildlife is also negatively affected by the loss of natural habitat. Farming and living closer to the rivers often lead to greater pollution of water resources.

The best management strategy is to not develop floodplains. But this is also unrealistic. Floodplains have too much to offer to make them unusable. To end farming near rivers and lakes would lead to a decline in the food supply and an increase in prices. In this day of increased mobility, it is also unrealistic to think that we could stop paving new roads.

Transportation by land and by river is also important to the food market and national economy.

The next step is to floodproof what has been developed and limit any further development. Floodproofing can be done by raising buildings above the flood levels, constructing flood barriers, or in extreme cases move developments off floodplains. In its report to the Administration Floodplain Management Task Force, the Interagency Floodplain Management Review committee writes, "The federal government must set the example in floodplain management activities. . . . State and local governments must have a fiscal stake in floodplain management; without this stake, few incentives exist for them to be fully involved in floodplain management." The federal government has made it a habit to take the responsibility of caring for everyone during times of disaster. Management concerns have also been different at the federal, state, and local levels. They each want to protect their varying interests—the nation having to protect the country while the local government watches out for just a small section. The time has come for state and local governments as well as individuals to start taking responsibility for their own actions and working toward common goals for floodplain management. This means doing everything possible to prevent flood damages by taking the initiative to protect and manage floodplains so we do not hand our problems on to someone else, but deal with them in a manner that will be economically, socially, and ecologically beneficial for all.

The Galloway Report

Stacy Monge

In some ways the flood of 1993 did the nation a favor. It brought to the nation's attention the desperate need for change in the way government and the people handle floods and manage floodplains. The federal government put together a review committee to research the flood and floodplain management practices along the Mississippi River and its tributaries. Their research resulted in a 200-page "blueprint for change" titled *Sharing the Challenge: Floodplain Management into the 21st Century*.

In a letter to the Floodplain Management Task Force, Brigadier General Gerald E. Galloway of the Army Corps of Engineers wrote, "The thesis of the report is straightforward. Floods will continue to occur. The goals for floodplain management are clear. The means to carry out effective floodplain management exist today but need improvement and refocusing. It is now time to organize a national effort to conduct effective and efficient floodplain management. It is time to share responsibility and accountability for accomplishing floodplain management among all levels of government and with the citizens of the nation." The federal government has gotten into the habit of taking care of its citizens by paying for disasters, whether or not precautions were taken to prevent the disaster. This practice costs U.S. taxpayers billions of dollars. In order to alleviate these costs, state and local governments must take more responsibility for effective floodplain management, the National Flood Insurance Program must be reviewed and restructured so that more people participate in the program, and citizens must be better educated in floodplain management so that they may take an active role in protecting their communities from further devastation.

One of the biggest hindrances to effective and efficient floodplain management is that state and local governments have had very little at stake financially. Once the President declared the flood a national disaster, people knew that most of the damage would be taken care of by the federal government, and it has been. Minnesota alone has received $573.5 million so far. The figures continue to rise as damages have been further assessed. This practice has allowed states, counties, cities, and citizens to take a less active role in floodplain management than they should. "State and local governments must have a fiscal stake in floodplain management; without this stake, few incentives exist for them to be fully involved in floodplain management." In order to achieve this goal, it is necessary to better define the roles and responsibilities of each level of government. The committee suggested that the federal government set an example by enacting a national "Floodplain Management Act to define governmental responsibilities, strengthen federal-state coordination and assure accountability." This act would establish national guidelines and goals for state and local governments, put the responsibility for effective management in the hands of the states, and take federal support away from those who choose not to follow sound management practices. Federal assistance would be mainly technical, and monetary support would supplement state funds.

The ideal situation would be to move those already living within highly flooded areas to drier ground and to stop the development on floodplains. This would require fed-

Inundated home north of Marshall
   –Jerry Sowden,
   Marshall Independent

eral agencies to re-evaluate their present policies and programs. Many programs currently in place promote the development of floodplains. Many state and local governments allow development because it broadens the tax base. Agriculturally, floodplains are invaluable because they contain some of the most fertile soils. No development is therefore

a hard goal to reach. If the federal government is able to set the example the rest will follow.

Another area of concern is the National Flood Insurance Program (NFIP). Communities, such as Marshall, that participate in the program are required to meet specific national guidelines for floodplain management. New buildings must be built at least one foot above the 100-year flood level or they must be made floodproof by any number of means. If the requirements are met, the community residents are then allowed the option of purchasing flood insurance. If the community fails to meet the standards after granted participation in the program, all residents are in jeopardy of losing their insurability. The NFIP discourages floodplain development by making it more expensive to live in highly flooded areas. Federal Insurance Rate Maps outlining the 100- and 500-year flood levels are produced to serve as a guideline for insurance costs. Those living in an area designated as a 100-year flood boundary would pay higher premiums than those living in a 500-year flood boundary.

One of the shortcomings of the NFIP is that it sets only minimal standards for floodplain management that alone may not improve on damages caused by floods or discourage development within the 100-year flood level. It is up to the state and local governments to set higher standards if necessary to promote safe and reasonable development. The NFIP has a Community Rating System currently in place that "provides discounts on flood insurance premiums in those communities that have floodplain management programs above and beyond NFIP minimum requirements." The premium discounts help to promote better management, but more is needed to encourage widespread community participation.

One of the key factors to improving floodplain management is interagency and intergovernmental cooperation. The federal government has set guidelines for federal, state, and local governments to follow regarding floodplain management. It is then the responsibility of each unit to follow or improve on the established guidelines. Each agency or governing body can alter or add regulations as new and unique situations arise, but there is no uniform method of setting standards. This leads to many conflicts of interest among the various agencies, governments, and other interested parties. Therefore, little progress is often made toward effective measures of management. Problems may be the result of conflicting federal guidelines or programs that are not as efficient as state or local standards. As a rule of thumb, the stricter guidelines are followed, whether they be federal, state, or local.

Successful floodplain management has to begin at the local level. The nation is too big for the federal government to be everywhere at once guiding each community. Local governments and citizens should take a more active role in defining what is best for the future of floodplain management in their communities. The state government should help communities by setting clear standards and helping to enforce the guidelines. Alternatives to developing floodplains should be sought to alleviate unnecessary suffering due to flooding as well as to save taxpayers money during times of disaster. We do not appreciate paying for disasters that occur elsewhere so we should not expect those not affected by flooding to pay for our problems.

Eat Dessert First

Bill Holm

An old friend of mine died of AIDS a few years ago, surrounded by his friends, but ostracized by his family—a story too regular in America to tell again. He was cremated and then scattered in a place he loved. A year later a couple of his friends, both from Minneota, decided that he needed a stone with his name somewhere on this planet, so they ordered one for him from the Echo Granite Works. They instructed the carver to inscribe, along with his name, a favorite saying: "Eat dessert first; life is short and uncertain." They told the stoneworks, after spring thaw, to set the stone on a small hill next to the Yellow Medicine River, overlooking a large and remarkable garden.

The winter—long, nasty and regular—passed, but when the snow melted, the rain started. It rained some, then some more, then a lot, then drizzle, then gray damp cold, then more rain. Farmers waited, gardeners waited. For all any of us know, God waited. The music of the sump pump sang day and night along the Yellow Medicine, gurgling gloomy electric tunes in a long futile drone.

Basements turned into stagnant pools, yards into sloughs, beanfields into lakes, little creeks into the Minnesota; the Minnesota turned into the Amazon, looking as if it were about to swallow whole counties. Maybe the ocean was coming back—another pliestocene—new water lizards the size of tractors. Maybe if the moon ever came out full again in a black sky, the tide would start sloshing back and forth toward Dakota. Before and after aerial maps of rivers looked like arteries with angioplasty balloons exploded inside them.

Meanwhile, the black gravestone, now carved, sat in Echo, waiting. The river garden was transformed to a lake bottom, and you could canoe over the ghosts of tulips, irises, moonflowers, roses, daisies, violets, their shadowy beds drowned by ten feet of muddy brown water. The hilltop turned into a small spongy island, a long dirty swim from the still unflooded county road. The stone rested a whole year, now unwanted even by nature—as if nature itself had become the harsh family, passing judgment.

Tourists came from England to western Minnesota and photographed the black humor of local signs: *Prime Commercial Real Estate. Ready for Development. Phone* . . . with an edgeless panorama of water glubbing around it, or *Adopt A Highway—Singles for Christ* drowned in a ditch. And the rains went on, and on. Farmers with gamblers' souls went back to the bank for another dip to plant another late try at a crop. They lost; more rain fell.

It was a dead year—for everyone, even the dead with their unset stones. Rumors and theories drifted through coffee shop talk: weird ocean currents, volcanic eruptions in the Philippines, misguided cloud seeding, God arriving with fire and flood to judge and punish the quick and the dead. But, as usual in Minnesota, the disaster passed, the sun came out by winter, blizzards howled, the mercury plunged and then spring came, mild and dry and fine. Some lived, some died; some went broke, others shrugged. Only chance to blame.

And now the time of the black gravestone comes around again. The granite works sends a truck to Minneota on the day after the only heavy rain of an otherwise quiet year. The road to the river garden is a clot of mud. Where to put it? Put it among the Lutherans for awhile, I say. Maybe they'll like the motto and take heart from it. So there it sits, not where it's supposed to go at all, a creature of chance, misadventure, the flood of the century, the power of the sky and moving water and luck to do as they please with human affairs. "Eat dessert first; life is short and uncertain." Maybe that's what big floods teach us.

Essay on Sources

Rebecca Schlorf

For an overview of the nature and effects of the 1993 national flood, see Jerry Alder, "Troubled Waters," _Newsweek,_ July 26, 1994, 21–26; Larry A. Larson, "Tough Lessons from Recent Floods," _USA Today,_ July 1994, 33–35; Richard E. Sparks and Ruth Sparks, "After Floods: Restoring Ecosystems," _USA Today,_ July 1994, 40; Jack Williams, "The Great Flood," _Weatherwise,_ February–March 1994, 18–23.

For two useful photographic books on the 1993 floods, see _St. Louis Post-Dispatch, High and Mighty_ (Kansas City, Mo.: Andrews and McMeel, 1993), and Mike Wegner, ed., _Iowa's Lost Summer_ (Iowa: Iowa State University Press and the Des Moines Register and Tribune Company, 1993).

For a view of the 1993 floods in southwestern Minnesota, see Minnesota Agricultural Statistics Service, _1993 Minnesota Weekly Crop-Weather Report_ (St. Paul: Crop and Livestock Reporting Service, 1993); Minnesota Agricultural Statistics Service, _1994 Minnesota Weekly Crop-Weather Report_ (St. Paul: Crop and Livestock Reporting Service, 1994); Minnesota Agricultural Statistics Service, _Minnesota Agricultural Statistics 1994_ (St. Paul: Crop and Livestock Reporting Service, 1994). Also see newspaper articles from: _Balaton Press Tribune, Canby News, Des Moines Register, Jackson County Pilot, Marshall Independent, Murray County News, Montevideo American News, Pipestone County Star, Redwood Gazette, Tracy Headlight Herald, Tri-County News,_ and _Worthington Daily Globe._

For the topography, hydrology, and water management of southwestern Minnesota, see Greg Breining, "Is the Mississippi Dying?" _The Minnesota Volunteer,_ November–December 1994, 8–19; Ferris Chamberlain, _The Great Flood of 1993 Post-Flood Report: Upper Mississippi River Basin_ (U.S. Army Corps of Engineers, 1994), Appendix A; Richard J. Chorely, ed., _Water, Earth and Man_ (London: Methuen and Co. Ltd., 1969); R. Victor, et al., _Flood Geomorphology_ (New York: John Wiley and Sons, Inc., 1988); Thomas F. Waters, _The Streams and Rivers of Minnesota_ (Minneapolis: University of Minnesota Press, 1977).

For a history and background on flooding in southwestern Minnesota and Marshall, see F. Case and A. P. Rose, _History of Lyon County, Minnesota, 1884–1912_ (Marceline, Mo.: Walsworth, 1977); Lyle K. Linch, _The History of the Pipestone Indian Shrine and National Monument_ (n.p.: 1954); Robert A. Murray, _A History of Pipestone National Monument, Minnesota_ (Pipestone, Minn.: Pipestone Indian Shrine Association, 1965); National Hazards Research and Applications Information Center, _Floodplain Management in the United States: An Assessment Report_ (Boulder, Colo.: University of Colorado, 1992); Todd Snyder, "Troubled Waters: An Examination of Marshall Minnesota's Flood Problems," Senior Seminar History Paper, Southwest State University, Marshall, Minn., 1993; N. H. Winchell, _The Geology of Rock and Pipestone Counties_ (Minneapolis: Johnson, Smith, and Harrison, 1878).

For an introduction to the diverse agencies and their reports and roles in the 1993 flood, see *Disaster Response and Recovery: Request Procedures Relative to State and Federal Disaster Assistance Programs* (St. Paul: Minnesota Department of Public Safety, 1993); *The Great Flood of 1993: The Minnesota Experience* (St. Paul: Minnesota Department of Public Safety, 1994); *Water, Water, Everywhere: Minnesota Flooding 1993* (St. Paul: Minnesota Department of Natural Resources, 1994); *Sharing the Challenge: Floodplain Management into the 21st Century,* Report of the Interagency Floodplain Management Review Committee to the Administration Floodplain Management Task Force

(Washington, D.C.: Government Printing Office, 1994); *Natural Disaster Survey Report: The Great Flood of 1993* (Washington, D.C.: Government Printing Office, 1994).

For reactions, policies, and ensuing debate of the 1993 flood in southwestern Minnesota and the nation see Harry E. Kitch, "Limiting the Impact of Future Floods," *USA Today,* July 1994, 36–39; *Sanitary Sewer Evaluation Study (Bruce Street System)* (St. Paul: Short Elliott Hendrickson Inc., 1994); Malcolm Simmons, *A Descriptive Analysis of Federal Relief, Insurance, and Loss Reduction Programs for Natural Hazards,* 94–195 ENR (Washington, D.C.: Congressional Research Service, 1994).

Biographies

Joseph A. Amato, the Flood Recovery Project Director, is the Director of Rural Studies and a Professor of History at Southwest State University (SSU). He is a regional and national writer whose publications include *When Father and Son Conspire, The Great Jerusalem Artichoke Circus, Servants of the Land,* and *The Decline of Rural Minnesota.*

Janet Timmerman is a graduate of SSU with a B.A. in History and is working towards a B.A. in Art. She is the author of an essay, "Draining the Great Oasis," which is included in the Society for the Study of Local and Regional History and SSU Rural Studies and History Department's "Rural Essay Series."

Toni Beebout-Bladholm is a senior at SSU majoring in English and Speech Secondary Education. She resides with her husband Mark in Marshall.

Jennifer Mathiason, from Walnut Grove, is a senior majoring in Literature/Creative Writing at SSU.

Stacy Monge is a graduate of Gustavus Adolphus College and holds a B.A. in Philosophy. She is currently working towards a degree in Elementary Education at SSU.

Julie Porter of Austin, Minnesota, is a graduate of Winona State University with a B.A. in Art. She is currently working towards a degree in History and Art Education.

Rebecca Schlorf, from Cottage Grove, Minnesota, is a junior at SSU majoring in Biology, with an emphasis on Environmental Biology.

Guest Contributors:

Bill Holm is, as locals say, from Minneota, and still lives there. When he is not teaching in the English Department at Southwest State University, he works on his books, and on improving his keyboard skills. He has published six books, both prose and poetry, most recently *The Dead Get By With Everything* and *Landscape of Ghosts.*

Janet Liebl is a 1994 graduate of Southwest State University. She holds a degree in History and a Secondary Education license in Social Science. She is the author of "Ties That Bind: The Orphan Train Story in Minnesota" which was published as part of the SSU Rural Studies and History Department's Historical Essay Series. Currently she is teaching Social Science at Dawson-Boyd High School.

Howard Mohr is the author of *How To Tell A Tornado, How To Talk Minnesotan,* and *A Minnesota Book of Days (And A Few Nights).*

Jim Muchlinski is a 1990 graduate of SSU and has worked as a staff writer at the *Marshall Independent* since 1991. Originally from Marshall, Jim covers the region's farm sector and a group of area communities. After covering the floods of 1993, he assisted the Flood Recovery Project as a consultant.

David Pichaske, a professor of English at Southwest State, lives beside the public access on the Minnesota River south of Granite Falls, with his wife Michelle and dogs Dylan and

Bear. Dr. Pichaske has published a number of books, including *Late Harvest: Recent Rural American Writing, A Generation in Motion: Music and Culture in the Sixties,* and *Poland in Transition: 1989–1991.*

CHARLES K. PIEHL is an Associate Professor of History at Mankato State University. He is the author of several articles on American history and is currently at work researching the Great Flood of 1927.